Acing Your First Year of Law School

Eight Secrets at
Top Exam.
Performance in
Law School
Charles A. Whitehead

# Acing Your First Year of Law School:
✦ The Ten Steps to Success
You Won't Learn in Class

*by*
Shana Connell Noyes
*&*
Henry S. Noyes

Fred B.
Rothman & Co.
Littleton, Colorado 80127
1999

*Library of Congress Cataloging-in-Publication Data*

Noyes, Shana Connell.
  Acing your first year of law school : the ten steps to success you
won't learn in class / by Shana Connell Noyes & Henry S. Noyes.

       p.    cm.

  Includes index.
  ISBN 0-8377-0913-X (alk. paper). — ISBN 0-8377-0912-1
(pbk. : alk. paper)
  1. Law—United States—Study and teaching.  2. Law students
—United States—Handbooks, manuals, etc.  I. Noyes, Henry S.
II. Title.
KF283.N69  1999
340'.071'173—dc21                                    99-13986
                                                        CIP

2nd printing 2001

Printed in the United States of America

This volume is printed on acid-free paper.

Fred B. Rothman Publications

*a division of*
William S. Hein & Co., Inc.
Buffalo, New York

# ✦ Table of Contents

# ✦ About the Authors

Both Shana and Henry Noyes made law review based on their first-year grades and in 1994 graduated in the top three percent of their classes. They both earned judicial clerkships with federal appellate judges and went on to join a prominent law firm. While in law school, Shana worked as consultant to Julia Roberts and director Alan J. Paluka on the film *The Pelican Brief.* Henry now practices commercial litigation with one of California's oldest law firms, Pillsbury Madison & Sutro LLP, and Shana writes full time.

# ✦ The Socratic Method And How to Beat It

Law school is notorious. Of all the graduate schools you could have chosen, you chose the one with the reputation for being the worst. And of all the three years of law school, the first year is more difficult than the other two years combined. Why is that?

Many factors will contribute to your stress level in law school, but there are three main reasons why your first year will be worse than any other year.

For starters, your first year is by far the most important year of law school. The one piece of advice that all graduated law students have for incoming first years is to work as hard as you can your first year, because your first-year grades follow you not just throughout law school but far into your legal career. Those grades determine whether you will earn a place on the Law Review or Moot Court, whether you will get a job as a summer associate your first and second summers and whether you will get a judicial clerkship after graduation. Because so much is riding on these grades, it's impossible to undo the damage done by a bad set of first-year grades. From the first day of law school, the pressure is on you to do the very best you can.

It's difficult to do the best you can, however, because of the second reason: You know little if anything about the study of law. Law school is not an extension of your undergraduate work; it is unlike anything you've ever done before. You don't know how to read or brief a case, do legal research or write legal memoranda, outline your classes or write exam answers.

This leads us to the third reason why the first year of law school is worse than the other two years combined: Because no one will teach you what you don't know. Let us repeat: No one will teach you how to perform any of the skills you need to study the law. You will have to teach yourself. This is called the "Socratic Method," and nearly every law school in the country follows this method of teaching. You can think of the Socratic Method like Darwin's Theory of Natural Selection: Only the strong survive. The strong are the students who somehow manage to teach themselves through trial and error the skills they need to study the law, and they are the ones who rise to the top of the class. Those who take longer to figure out how to perform these skills find themselves in the middle or at the bottom of the class. Unless you know how to perform the skills necessary to study the law, you will not excel in your first year of law school, no matter how much you study or how hard you work. The bottom line is that if you're going to do well in law school, you're going to have to beat the Socratic Method.

This book will show you how. In ten chapters, this book teaches you the skills you need to know to study the law. They are how to:

+ Read a case
+ Brief a case
+ Learn from Socratic Class discussion
+ Do legal research
+ Do legal writing
+ Navigate the *Bluebook* of legal citation
+ Use study aids effectively
+ Prepare outlines for each class
+ Study for exams, and
+ Write exam answers.

It's a lot to learn. But to make the task easier on you, this book also tells you what you do *not* need to know and should not waste time worrying about. Most first years waste a tremendous amount of time learning piles of information they don't need to know, because they have no one to guide them. To save you that time, each chapter of this book ends with a list of things you do not need to worry about so that you can spend your time wisely studying what you do need to learn. Lawyers have a word for things that are unimportant: The word is "dicta." Every chapter of this book ends with a "Dicta Column" which lists for you the unimportant things that you will run across during your first year but should not study nor waste your time worrying about.

Your first year of law school is not going to be easy. You know that. But you can beat the Socratic Method and ace your first year of law school. This book will show you how.

# CHAPTER ONE
## ✦ How to Read a Case

The first thing you need to learn as you start law school is how to read a case. The backbone of the Socratic Method is casebook reading, and you will read thousands of cases throughout your law school career. Casebooks are your textbooks, and cases are where you will find the rules, theories and doctrines of law that you will need to know for your final exams.

Unfortunately, cases are not easy to read, especially for first years, and learning to read cases can be a difficult process. Cases are full of legal terms and concepts you've never seen before. They have an odd format. Because every case you'll read is written by a different judge, there's no consistency to them. Many cases have complicated subject matter and use questionable logic. Quite a few are badly written. Finally and most importantly, it is the extremely rare case that will serve you up clear-cut rules of law that you can write down and memorize. Instead, cases require you to go a step further; you must not only read cases, but analyze and extract from them specific theories and concepts and rules of law.

This chapter will give you some perspective on cases—where they come from and where they fit in the American legal system—because to understand their content, you need to know how they function in our legal system. In this chapter you will learn about:

I.   Where cases come from
II.  Civil and criminal cases
III. Federal and state court systems
IV.  Precedent
V.   Majority and dissenting opinions
VI.  Procedural history
VII. Case citations
VIII. The role cases play in the Socratic Method
IX.  How to read your casebooks

1

# I. Where Cases Come From

The cases in your casebook are real cases that were decided by a court at some time, somewhere. A judge or justice wrote a legal opinion which was then published in a "reporter of cases." Every published legal opinion, or case, becomes part of the American "common law," a collective term for all the cases American courts decide. The colonists from England brought the common law system with them when they settled America, and all but one state, Louisiana, follow the common law system. Louisiana is a civil law state with laws derived from the French civil law. Louisiana laws are codified, or collected, in a book called the *Louisiana Civil Code*. Although the legal system in Louisiana is slightly different than in the rest of the country, the process of reading cases is the same no matter where in the country you go to law school or practice law.

# II. Civil and Criminal Cases

A civil action is any action brought to enforce private rights or redress private injury. Civil actions include all cases that are not criminal cases. Criminal cases are brought against persons charged with violating the criminal laws. There are different rules of procedure governing civil and criminal actions.

# III. Federal and State Courts

There are two court systems in America, federal and state. As you go through law school you will learn the intricacies of the federal and state court systems and the kinds of cases they hear. For now, you need only have a very general idea about these courts. Be aware that the following rules are general rules and that there are exceptions to these general rules. This overview is meant only to give you a basic idea about American courts of law so that when you hear your professors talk about these courts, you'll have some idea of what's going on.

## A. Federal Courts

There are three main types of courts in the federal system: district courts, circuit courts and the United States Supreme Court.

### 1. District Courts

District courts are federal trial courts, the first place parties go to settle a dispute. District courts hear both civil and criminal cases, and one judge presides over the proceedings. Witnesses are called, sworn in, questioned and cross-examined. If the case is a jury trial, the jury resolves the factual disputes and renders the "verdict" in a criminal case or the "judgment" in a civil case. If the case is tried without a jury, it is called a "bench trial" and the judge resolves the factual disputes and renders the verdict or judgment.

### 2. Circuit Courts

Circuit courts are federal courts of appeal. These courts are called circuit courts because the United States is divided into thirteen sections, called "circuits," each with its own judges. Circuit courts hear appeals from several district courts. Every circuit contains three or more states, except for the District of Columbia, which is its own circuit called the D.C. Circuit, and the Federal Circuit, which handles patent cases.

Parties who are unhappy with the district court's decision can go to the circuit court to appeal the decision. Circuit courts operate differently from district courts. In general, three judges sit on a panel to decide the case based entirely on the evidence the district court had before it. No jury is empaneled and no witnesses are called. The attorneys from both sides submit "appellate briefs" for the panel to read and sometimes make arguments to the three-judge panel. The circuit court's job is to determine whether the district court correctly decided the case. Circuit courts do not reconsider questions of fact such as whether witnesses were telling the truth when they testified. Instead, circuit courts consider questions of law; they decide only whether the district court applied the law correctly in deciding the case. When a case is very important, all the judges of the circuit sit on a panel to decide the case. This is called sitting "en banc."

### 3. United States Supreme Court

The United States Supreme Court is the highest court in the country, the end of the line in terms of appeals. The Court (always capitalized) has the final say on all questions of federal law and questions involving the U.S. Constitution. The nine men and women who sit on the Supreme Court are called "justices," not judges. While the Supreme Court does have original jurisdiction in some cases (meaning that it acts as a trial court rather than an appeals court), the Supreme Court acts most often as an appeals court.

Unlike other appeals courts, the Court generally has discretion whether to hear appeals from lower courts. When a party seeks to appeal a case to the Supreme Court, it is called "filing for certiorari." The Court can either grant or deny certiorari, or "cert." A denial of certiorari may be an indication that the Court agrees with the decision of the lower court (usually a circuit court), but it can also mean that the Court does not consider the case important enough for reconsideration. A grant of certiorari, on the other hand, means that the Court considers the case worthy of its attention.

When the Court hears cases, all nine justices sit on a panel and hear arguments from the attorneys representing each party. The justices ask the attorneys questions and read the briefs submitted. There is no jury and no witnesses are called. Once the Court issues an opinion, that's it. The opinion is the law, until and unless the Court changes its mind by overruling its prior decision or Congress changes the law by enacting legislation.

## B. State Courts

Each state has different names for their courts, which include everything from small claims courts to municipal courts and traffic courts to appeals courts to a state supreme court. Most state court systems, however, have a three-level structure that is very similar to the federal system.

### 1. Trial Courts

Trial courts are where parties go first to settle a dispute. As in federal court, one judge presides, witnesses are called and a jury may or may not be empaneled to render a verdict or judgment. Unlike federal court, however, state trial courts often have separate systems for civil and criminal cases.

### 2. Appeals Courts

As in circuit courts, appeals courts are where the party who lost in the trial court goes to appeal the decision. No witnesses are called and no jury is empaneled. Again, like circuit courts, appeals courts do not decide questions of fact. The appeals court's task is to decide whether the trial court correctly applied the law to decide the case.

### 3. State Supreme Court

The state supreme court is the highest state court, and it hears appeals from the state appeals courts. State supreme courts have varying numbers of justices. Again, no witnesses are called and no jury is empaneled. Decisions of a state supreme court involving issues of federal law or the U.S. Constitution can be appealed to the United States Supreme Court. Purely state law issues, however, cannot be appealed to the U.S. Supreme Court, because a state supreme court has the final word on issues of state law. Its opinion is the law until and unless the court changes its mind and overrules a prior decision or the state legislature changes the law by enacting legislation.

# IV. The Concept of Precedent

When a court makes a decision in a case, the decision is binding on that court in all factually identical cases that arise in the future. This is the concept of *stare decisis*. The initial decision is called "precedent," and precedent continues to influence subsequent cases unless the court which decided the case determines that the decision was wrong and reverses itself or a higher court reverses or vacates the decision. Precedent is binding on both the court that made the initial decision and to varying degrees on other courts. The general rule is that the higher the court, the more binding its decisions.

## A. Federal Court

The decisions of the United States Supreme Court are binding on all courts, state and federal. Decisions of circuit courts are binding on that circuit court and all of the district courts within that circuit. While one circuit's decisions are not binding outside the circuit, they are "persuasive authority" on the decisions of other circuits. When two separate circuits disagree over the outcome of a legal question, it is called a "circuit split" and the United States Supreme Court often grants certiorari to settle the dispute.

## B. State Court

Decisions of a state supreme court are binding on all courts in that state. State appeals courts decisions are binding on the appeals courts and all lower courts in that state. State trial court decisions are binding only on that trial court. One state can, of course, have laws different from those in other states. For example, gambling is legal in Nevada but illegal in most other states.

# V. Opinions: Majority, Dissenting, Concurring, and Plurality

## A. Majority Opinions

In trial courts, both state and federal, there is usually only one decision—a verdict or judgment—that is rendered by the jury in a jury trial or the judge in a bench trial. In appeals courts more than one judge hears cases, and the judges vote to decide those cases. Each judge has one vote, and majority wins. The decision of the majority is the "majority opinion," and that decision of the court becomes precedent.

## B. Dissenting Opinions

When more than one judge decides a case, such as the panel of three or whole circuits that decide federal appeals cases, there is always the possibility that judges will disagree. The same is true for state supreme courts and for the United States Supreme Court. Every judge or justice has an equal vote, and when they disagree over the outcome of a case, they may decide to write more than one opinion.

Take a circuit court, for example. Because majority always wins, if two of the three circuit judges on a panel agree and the third judge disagrees, the decision of the two judges is the decision of the court, because the two are a majority. The majority opinion is precedent for future cases. The third judge who disagreed with the majority has the option to write what is called a "dissenting opinion," where she can vent her disagreement with the majority and explain why she thinks the majority is wrong. This dissenting opinion, however, is not the decision of the court and has no precedential value. A dissent is just a forum where the judge who disagrees can explain why she disagrees. Even though dissenting opinions do not become precedent, you will read dissenting opinions in law school because they show you how courts can use different reasoning to decide the correct outcome of a case.

## C. Concurring Opinions

Another kind of opinion is a "concurring opinion." A judge will write a concurring opinion when she agrees with the *decision* of the majority but not the *reasoning*. In such a case, the disagreeing judge writes a separate concurring opinion to explain her reasons for coming to the decision she did, which are different from the majority's reasoning.

## D. Plurality Opinions

Another kind of opinion is the "plurality opinion." You will read many plurality opinions issued by the United States Supreme Court. After the Court hears a case and before it issues an opinion, the justices discuss the case and give their view of what the outcome should be. When the justices have different views, they negotiate with each other in an effort to band into a majority that can express the opinion of the Court. If a majority of the justices cannot reach agreement, the greatest number of agreeing justices join to deliver the decision of the Court, called a plurality opinion. For example, four justices may join one opinion, three others join a second opinion, and the last two justices join a third opinion. The opinion is then called a plurality opinion, not a majority opinion, because the decision did not command a majority of the Court.

# VI. Procedural History

The procedural history of a case is the route a case traveled to get to the court that produced the opinion you are reading. When you see something like "plaintiff filed the suit in federal court, the district court found for the defendant, the plaintiff appealed, the appeals court reversed and remanded the case back to the district court," that's procedural history. Sometimes cases have very long and confusing procedural history, but do not let this overly concern you. You will learn more about procedural history in Civil Procedure class, because Civil Procedure is about procedure. But do not worry about memorizing procedural history, because even in civil procedure, chances are that no exam question will ask you to remember the procedural history of a particular case.

The only time you need to concern yourself with procedural history is for class discussion. When a case has a particularly confusing procedural history, professors like to call on students to explain it. If this happens to you, refer to your casebook and try to answer the professor's questions. Once class is over, however, don't give it any more thought because it is very unlikely that you'll be required to know the procedural history of that case again.

# VII. Case Citations

Immediately following the name of every case in your casebook is the "case citation," which includes numbers, an abbreviation and a date, such as "424 U.S. 382 (1976)." These citations tell you what court wrote the opinion, what date the case was decided and where you can find a particular case in the "case reporters." Most cases are printed in more than one reporter, and that is why you will often see citations listing the two reporters in which a particular case appears.

Federal cases are reported in the federal reporters. District court decisions appear in reporters called the *Federal Supplement*, abbreviated as "F. Supp." and "F. Supp. 2d." Circuit court decisions appear in the *Federal Reporter*, abbreviated as "F.," "F.2d," or "F.3d". Decisions of the United States Supreme Court are reported in the *United States Reports*, abbreviated as "U.S." The *Federal Supplement, Federal Reporter* and *United States Reports* are all known as "official reporters." A private company also reports the decisions of the Supreme Court in the *Supreme Court Reporter*, abbreviated as "S. Ct."

State cases are reported in the state reporters. Most states have an official reporter that contains state court opinions. State court decisions also appear in what are called regional reporters. For example, decisions of the California Supreme Court are printed in the *California Reporter* and in the *Pacific Reports*, because California is in the Pacific region.

Case citations work the same way for all reporters, federal and state, official and unofficial. The volume in which a case appears comes before the name of the reporter, and the page on which the case begins comes after. For example, a case cited as 424 U.S. 382 (1976) appears in volume 424 of the *United States Reports* at page 382 and was decided by the U.S. Supreme Court in 1976.

# VIII. Cases and the Socratic Method

In the next chapter you will learn how to analyze cases and extract the four essential elements of every case: the facts, issue, legal reasoning and holding (or "rule of the case"). Before you begin analyzing cases, however, you need to understand the role cases play in the Socratic Method.

As you learned earlier in this chapter, the cases you will read in law school do not isolate and identify clear-cut rules of law that you can write down and memorize. Instead, you must not only read cases but also analyze and extract from them rules of law, legal theories and legal reasoning. Even the most simple and straightforward case requires thought and analysis and, unfortunately, hardly any of the cases that appear in your casebook are simple and straightforward.

The cases that earn a spot in your casebook are not your basic, run-of-the-mill cases that courts decide every day across the country. Instead, the cases that appear in your casebook are the difficult cases. To be included in a law school casebook, there must be something exceptional about a case that warrants memorializing it for students to study year after year. The theory of the Socratic Method is that by reading cases that stretch the limits of the law, you will stretch the limits of your analytic ability. The Socratic Method wants to produce a lawyer who is ready for anything, and if you read only cookie-cutter cases, those are the only kind of cases for which you will be prepared. The Socratic Method has you read the wildcard cases so that no matter what curve ball you're thrown, you can handle it.

With this understanding, hopefully you will find the cases in your casebook less intimidating. Don't expect your cases to be easy to understand. Every time you begin a new case, remember that the case is exceptional for some reason and try to figure out why. This sounds more difficult than it really is, because there are only four basic ways a case can be exceptional:

✦ *The case stands for a rule of law.* Either a brand-new rule of law is announced for the first time in that case or the case is such a perfect situation in which to apply the rule that the case warrants attention. These cases are the easy ones—easy to read, understand and remember.

✦ *The case modifies a rule of law by extending it to cover a new situation.* Most of the cases in your casebooks will fall into this category. Casebook editors choose these cases because they show you how the law changes a little, case by case, and goes in a new direction. The facts of these cases are not identical, but the court extends the rule of law to analogous situations. These cases are a good teaching tool because they show you how courts apply the law and reasoning of a prior decision to new and unforeseen facts to arrive at a decision. That is exactly what your final exams will ask you to do, and the more familiar you are with the process, the better prepared you'll be to answer your exam questions.

✦   *The case misapplies a rule of law.* These cases are the most difficult for first years, because you do not yet have the confidence to question the accuracy of a case in your casebook. Instead of questioning the case, your first reaction is to question your own ability to understand the case. These cases leave first years frustrated and confused.

If you are on the lookout for these cases, however, you can save yourself some frustration when you come across one. The way to spot the misapplies-a-rule case is this: Say you have read several cases in a particular area. You are comfortable with the legal concept the cases address and can see the progression of the law. Then, all of a sudden, you come upon a case that disregards everything you thought you understood. You try to come up with a reason why a rule of law was applied in a situation where you thought it shouldn't, but you can't. This is a red flag indicating that you've hit upon a case that was wrongly decided. If a case strikes you as simply wrong, it probably is. And if your professor calls on you in class to explain the case, have the confidence to give the right answer—that the case was wrongly decided.

✦   *The case is incomprehensible.* This is the least common type of case, but unless you are on the alert, it can be the most frustrating. Rarely, but sometimes, you will read a case that makes absolutely no sense. No matter how many times you read it, you have no idea what in the world is going on. It could be a strange old case from an archaic British court, or it could be a weird case dealing with a discrete area of Civil Procedure law. There are several cases famous among law students for making no sense at all, such as *Pennoyer v. Neff* and *Sibbach v. Wilson.* When you come across one of these cases, make an attempt to get some grasp on it, but don't do battle with it. Read a commercial outline to get some kind of understanding of the case, then move on. Just let it go. Chances are, the case is so odd you'll never be tested on it anyway.

Beware in class, however. These are the cases that professors like to talk to death, just to show all you first years how little you know. Your smartest move is to let the professor run with the ego trip and don't get bogged down or frustrated with the nonsensical case. It's not worth your time.

# IX. Deciding How to Read Your Casebooks

Everyone has a different opinion on how to read cases most effectively. Some people read cases only once, slowly. Some read cases twice, first slow then fast, or vice versa. Some people highlight as they go, some make notes in the margin, some draw little pictures by the case citation to help trigger their memory of the case.

Because everyone reads differently, you will have to decide what method works best for you. You may try several different reading methods before deciding on one that you like. As you develop your own style, keep in mind the following guidelines:

✦ *Do not skim*. Skimming is not an option. Cases do not lend themselves to cursory run-throughs. You must read cases from beginning to end.

✦ *Read actively*. You will spend a lot of time reading, and it is important to use that time wisely. Reading wisely is reading actively, and reading actively means being engaged in the case as you read it. As you read, visualize the parties and think about their dispute. Give your plaintiffs faces. Be involved in their fight. Cases are, above anything else, stories. As you read, visualize in your mind how the story plays out. Reading a case actively just once is far more beneficial to you than reading it three times with a blank stare and a blank mind.

✦ *Respect your reading speed*. If you are a fast reader, you may want to consider reading cases twice, at least at first. If you are a slower reader, however, you should not read cases more than once. Your reading assignments in law school will be enormous, and if you are a slower reader, you will not have time to read things twice. Do not fall behind in your reading. Your goal is to keep up with your assignments.

✦ *Beware of highlighters*. This does not mean you shouldn't use highlighters—just use them carefully. When students read and highlight at the same time, there's a tendency to skim or even skip over the words they're highlighting, and highlighting becomes a substitute for actually reading.

## ✦ Dicta Column

After the first few weeks of law school, most students feel overwhelmed. Everything is new and you feel like you will never be able to learn it all.

Worse, you know that even if you could fit everything into your brain, you don't have time to get it all in there.

Don't worry. This column is here to tell you that you don't have to learn it all. One of the most valuable skills you will learn in law school is how to determine what is important and what is not. The only way to learn that skill, however, is experience. So for now, this column will take the place of experience and tell you what you do not need to know.

✦ *Do not memorize case names.* Some case names will just stick in your mind, but you do not need to worry about memorizing the names of the cases you read. Why? Because you do not need to know case names on your final exams. You need to know the rules embodied in the cases, but you do not need to know the case names.

✦ *Do not memorize case citations.* In fact, do not do anything more than look over case citations. As you start a new case, you should glance at the case citation to find out what court issued the opinion and when it was decided. You do not need to remember this information, however. The only reason to read the citation is to get a hint of what you're in for with that particular case. If the case is from the Supreme Court, you know the opinion probably will be long. If it's from 1792, you know you're in for a struggle—the language will be arcane and the legal concepts outdated.

✦ *Do not get ahead in your reading.* Your goal should be to keep up with your reading assignments, and that's all. Reading ahead is an affirmatively bad idea for two reasons. First, by the time your professor gets around to discussing the case, you will have forgotten it. Second, professors often change reading assignments at the last minute, and you do not want to find yourself having spent three hours reading an assignment that the professor later canceled. Just try to keep up with your assignments. If you manage to do that, you'll be doing better than many of your classmates.

✦ *Do not worry about archaic legal terms.* As you begin your reading assignments, you will probably come across references to archaic legal terms. Professors sometimes assign cases from the seventeenth century just to scare you, but you have nothing to fear. Don't worry if you run across phrases that you don't understand, such as replications, rejoinders, surrejoinders, assumpsit, and trials by ordeal, oath and batter. You don't have to memorize these terms. Sometimes professors throw these terms around to show off, and sometimes students actually take the time to learn what they mean, but the truth is, these terms generally don't matter and will never be on a final exam.

CHAPTER TWO
# ✦ How to Brief a Case

Early on in the semester, your professors will advise you that you need to brief every case you read. Your law school might even offer a seminar where you can learn how to write case briefs. Many students, however, will ignore this advice and decide not to do case briefs. They think that briefing's not worth the time.

They're wrong. Case briefing is worth the time. Case briefing is an essential, fundamental building block that you will use over and over again during your entire legal career. If you want to do well in your first year of law school, you have to brief your cases. It's true that case briefing will take up a great deal of your time your first year, but it is time well spent. Nothing teaches you more about learning to study the law than briefing cases. Briefing trains you how to read cases and break them down into their essential elements. When you get called on in class, case briefs help you answer your professor's questions. Most importantly, case briefs are invaluable when you outline your classes and study for exams.

The other good news about briefing is that you don't have to do it forever. After your first year, you won't write formal case briefs ever again. Why? Because briefing cases conscientiously during your first year trains you to brief cases in your mind as you read them. Intuitively, as you read, you will pick out the essential elements of the case, analyze and organize them. And you will do all this without having to write down a thing—if you brief your cases your first year. This chapter will teach you how.

Briefing is different than the notes you took on your reading in college. In college, your professors first taught you rules and then used examples to show you how to apply those rules. Law school is exactly the opposite. In law school, your professors don't teach you the rules. Instead, they have you read cases (examples of how rules are applied), then ask you to glean from those cases what the rules being applied actually are. The rules you are looking for are surrounded by thoughts, observations and commentary that are extraneous to the core elements of the case: i.e., dicta. Your job when briefing cases is to separate the essential elements from the mass of dicta that surrounds those elements.

Again, this is the Socratic Method at work, requiring you to teach yourself how to separate the essential from the extraneous. Your professors do not spoon-feed you the rules you need to learn. Instead, you must read cases and figure out on your own what rules are being applied and how they cause the outcome in that case. Every time you brief a case you will do the same thing:

I.   Synthesize the reading
II.  Pick out the essential elements and write them in your own words in your brief

All cases contain the four following elements: a certain situation, or set of FACTS; a question that the situation presents, or ISSUE; the legal rules that apply in that situation and why those rules apply, or LEGAL REASONING; and what the outcome is once you apply the rules to the issue, or HOLDING. Every time you read a case, your task is to isolate these four elements, think about them, put them into your own words, and write them in your case brief. The four elements usually appear in cases in that order—facts, issue, reasoning, holding, and your briefs will follow that order.

The best way to learn how to brief is to actually brief a case. The rest of this chapter is an exercise that will take about half an hour to complete. When you have an uninterrupted half-hour, take out a sheet of notebook paper and a pen. Then read the case below, *Delair v. McAdoo,* a case that appears in most first-year Torts casebooks. Read *Delair* at the speed you usually read cases, and then we'll brief it.

<u>Delair v. McAdoo</u>
Supreme Court of Pennsylvania
Nov. 23, 1936.

KEPHART, Chief Justice.

Plaintiff brought an action in trespass to recover for damages to his person and property sustained as a result of a collision between his automobile and that owned by the defendant. The accident occurred when defendant, proceeding in the same direction as plaintiff, sought to pass him. As defendant drew alongside of plaintiff, the left rear tire of his car blew out, causing it to swerve and come into contact with the plaintiff's car. The latter's theory at trial was that defendant was negligent in driving with defective tires.

The jury found for plaintiff in the sum of $7,500. The court below granted defendant a new trial on the ground that the verdict was excessive, but refused his motion for judgment n.o.v. Its ruling on the latter motion is here for review.

The case presents but another factual situation presenting in terms of realities the abstract legal principle that the owner of a motor vehicle must exercise such care with respect to it as not to subject others to unreasonable risk of injury from its operation.

\*     \*     \*     \*     \*     \*

It has been held in other states that the question whether a particular person is negligent in failing to know that his tires are in too poor a condition for ordinary operation on the highways is a question of fact for the jury. Campbell v. Spaeth, 213 Wis. 162, 250 N.W. 394; Ragsdale v. Love, 50 Ga. App. 900, 178 S.E. 755, 756. In the instant case the testimony relative to the defect was as follows: A witness for the plaintiff stated that the tire "was worn pretty well through. You could see the tread in the tire—the inside lining." The witness later described this inside lining as the "fabric." The fact that the tire was worn through to and into the fabric over its entire area was corroborated by another witness. The repairman who replaced the tire which had blown out stated that he could see "the breaker strip" which is just under the fabric of a tire. This testimony was contradicted by the defendant.

\*     \*     \*     \*     \*     \*

We have in this state more than a million automobiles and trucks, approximately two for every three families. Their daily use over the highways is common, and requires a certain amount of knowledge of moveable parts, particularly the tires; it is imperative that a duty or standard of care be set up that will be productive of safety for other users of the highways. Any ordinary individual, whether a car owner or not, knows that when a tire is worn through to the fabric, its further use is dangerous and it should be removed. When worn through several plies, it is very dangerous for further use. All drivers must be held to a knowledge of these facts. An owner or operator cannot escape simply because he says he does not know. He must know. The hazard is too great to permit cars in this condition to be on the highway. It does not require opinion evidence to demonstrate that a trigger pulled on a loaded gun makes the gun a dangerous instrument when pointed at an individual, nor could one escape liability by saying he did not know it was dangerous. The use of a tire worn through to the fabric presents a similar situation. The rule must be rigid if millions are to drive these instrumentalities which in a fraction of a second may become instruments of destruction to life and property. There is no series of accidents more destructive or more terrifying in the use of automobiles than those which come from "blow-outs." The law requires drivers and owners of motor vehicles to know the condition of those parts which are likely to become dangerous where the flaws or faults would be disclosed by a reasonable inspection. It will assume they do know of the dangers ascertainable by such examination.

Order affirmed.

# I. Synthesize the Reading

Before you write anything down, take a minute to consider what the case is about. It's a dispute between two drivers over a car accident, right? When McAdoo's tire blew out, he ran into Delair's car. Delair then sued McAdoo. Delair is the plaintiff and McAdoo is the defendant.

Once you have a general idea what the case is about, look over the procedural history of the case. As you learned in Chapter One, procedural history is not terribly important, primarily because you will not be required to remember a case's procedural history on your final exams. If you get called on in class, however, your professor may grill you on the procedural history of the case you're discussing, and you'll need to have a general idea what it is.

You know Delair is an appeal before you even read the case, because the opinion is from the Supreme Court of Pennsylvania. In the first paragraph of the opinion you learn what happened in the trial court—the jury found for the plaintiff and awarded him $7500 damages. You also see that after the jury rendered this verdict, the judge granted the defendant a new trial because he thought the award was too high, but denied the defendant's motion for j.n.o.v., and the defendant appealed.

You should also note anything in the procedural history that you don't understand, such as "trespass" and "j.n.o.v." Your law dictionary will tell you that trespass is an old-fashioned word for a suit brought in tort, and j.n.o.v. stands for "judgment notwithstanding the verdict," which is exactly what it sounds like—a judgment notwithstanding the jury's verdict. In this case, the defendant asked the judge for judgment in his favor, notwithstanding the fact that the jury found for the plaintiff. That's as far as you need to go with procedural history. You will learn all about j.n.o.v. in your Civil Procedure class, so don't spend time worrying about it now.

# II. Pick Out the Essential Elements and Write Them in Your Own Words

Now that you have taken time to figure out generally what's going on in the case and the procedural history, take out a sheet of paper, write "Delair v. McAdoo" at the top of the page and underline it. A case brief is just what it says it is—brief—and your goal is to keep your case briefs as short as possible. Restrict them to one side of the page, if you can. One-page briefs are convenient for use in class and for the outlining you'll do later in the semester, they're neat and organized, and the truth is, most cases do not require more than one page of briefing. As you learned earlier in this chapter, your briefs will follow the order of the four essential elements of every case: facts, issue, reasoning, holding. To pick out those elements, you will need to go back to the case and re-read to determine what information should go in each category. Turn to the beginning of the case to find the first element, the facts.

## A. Facts

In the margin underneath the case name, write the word "Facts" and underline it. The first thing to remember about facts is not to argue with them. The facts of the cases you read are no longer in dispute. The trial court tried the facts and made a decision about them, and they're not going to change. In this case, the court found that the defendant hit the plaintiff's car. Take these facts as they are given to you. Getting caught up in whether the facts are true or whether the trial court made the correct determination of the facts is not your job. Your job is to summarize the facts as they are written in the case.

Now look over the facts of the case again, and before you write anything, think about what's going on. The point of briefing is to synthesize the reading, pick out the essential elements and put those elements in your brief in your own words. As you read, remember:

+ *Do not copy.* Even if you're tempted to copy directly from the case, don't. What kind of sentence is "Plaintiff brought an action in trespass to recover for damages to his person and property sustained as a result of a collision between his automobile and that owned by the defendant," anyway? Not the kind of sentence you want to copy.
+ *Do not be wordy.* Using legalese instead of plain old English does not make you sound like you know more, it just confuses you. Look again

at the sentence in the above paragraph. It's legalese for "Plaintiff sued Defendant after Defendant crashed into him." Plain English is easier to read, makes sense and shows that you understand what's going on. When you have the choice between using a simple word and a multi-syllable high-faluting word, always go for the simple one.

✦ *Have an opinion.* You should include in your case brief the observations you have on a particular case, if you have any. For instance, if you think a case comes to a bad decision, say so in your brief, and remember to include why you think that. Then if you get called on in class and your professor asks you to tell him what you think of the case, you'll be ready to give him an answer right away. Putting some thought into your case briefs will make them more useful to you both in class and when you make your outlines. Just remember to keep your comments short.

✦ *Think about what's really important.* It's common for first years to include much more information than they need in their case briefs. This is partially because you are just starting out and have no way to know what is important and what is not. It's also because it's easier to include everything than to take the time to decide what's important and what's not.

✦ *Take the time.* What's important in this case? Not much. Your facts section could go something like this: "Defendant's tire blew out and he crashed into Plaintiff's car. Plaintiff sued Defendant claiming Defendant was negligent for driving with bad tires. Jury found for Plaintiff, Defendant appealed." That's it. It doesn't seem like a lot, but what else is important? Does it matter that the Defendant was trying to pass the Plaintiff when the tire blew out? Not really. Does it matter that the Defendant swerved before he hit the Plaintiff? No. Does it matter that the jury awarded the Plaintiff the amount of $7,500? No. Who cares how much the jury awarded? It doesn't matter. If a fact isn't important, it doesn't go in your brief. The fewer facts the better. Take the time to decide what's important and what's not.

## B. Issue

Now move on to the issue. Write "Issue" in the margin under your facts and underline it. Now look back at the case to find the issue. Usually the issue is easy to spot; cases often say "the issue presented by these facts is . . ." or "in this case we consider the question of whether . . . ." The *Delair* court is not quite so specific, but if you are persistent and look where the issue usually appears (right after the facts) you will be able to spot it. You know from reading the case that the issue has something to do with negligence and bald tires. You even see a sentence that sounds like the issue, the one that begins "The case presents but another factual situation presenting in terms of realities the abstract legal principle that the owner of a motor vehicle must exercise such care . . ." This sentence sounds like the issue, but it's so convoluted that it wouldn't help you at all to paraphrase it. So what do you do?

Delair is more difficult than most other cases in that the issue is not stated in plain language in the case. This happens. And when it does, you need to develop and trust your ability to phrase the issue yourself. Your goal is to learn to define the issue clearly and simply. When there is no clear-cut statement of the issue in a case, make a reasonable stab at what you think the issue is. Issues are usually one sentence long, so write one sentence that states the general issue of the case. One way to state the issue in Delair is "Is it negligent to drive on bald tires?"

## C. Reasoning

When presented with a dispute, courts draw on two sources to decide the proper resolution: (1) established rules from other cases (precedent), and (2) theories of social policy. Remember from Chapter One that courts are required to apply precedent, because precedent controls the outcome of cases that arise after it. In addition to rules, courts can and often do use social policy considerations to make their decision, because those are the reasons why we have laws in the first place. Social policy asks the question of why we have a particular rule and what we are trying to accomplish as a society by having such a law.

Looking at Delair we see that the court used the following precedent to decide whether the Defendant was negligent for driving on faulty tires:

1.  People should know that when a tire is worn through it's dangerous to drive;
2.  We must assume that drivers do know that; and
3.  People can't escape responsibility for the damage faulty tires can cause just by claiming they didn't know the tires were worn.

The social policy arguments the Delair court considered are:

1.  With more than a million cars and trucks on the road, we need drivers to be held to a certain standard of care that will promote safety; and
2.  Because the danger is so great, we need a rigid rule that assumes people should inspect their cars and charges people with responsibility for the defects an inspection would reveal.

The Reasoning section in your brief will be the longest section, because the bulk of most cases is made up of legal reasoning. Also, you may be over-inclusive in this section, especially at first. Be patient with yourself and realize that with every case, you're learning more and more. Learning to glean the rules and social policy arguments from cases is extremely valuable to you, because these are the kinds of arguments you will be required to make on your final exams. Writing case briefs with thoughtful Reasoning sections is the best way to practice for writing exams.

## D. Holding

The Reasoning above leads the court to a conclusion, or a settlement of the dispute in the case. This is called the "holding." The holding is the opposite of dicta; whereas dicta is extraneous to the case and not binding as precedent, the holding is the very decision the case stands for and is binding precedent. The holding is sometimes called the "rule of the case," and that is the rule you must remember for your final exam. For example, if on your Torts exam you get a question involving a driver who has broken headlights and crashes into another car, you will use *Delair* in your answer. *Delair* involved a tire and your question is about headlights, but *Delair* applies, because *Delair* stands for the proposition that drivers have a duty to know their car's defects that are ascertainable by inspection, and if they drive with faulty cars, they are responsible for the damage they cause.

The most important thing to remember as you write the holding in your brief is that you must be neither too broad nor too narrow. The reasoning in *Delair* leads the court to hold that "drivers have a duty to keep their cars safe, and if they drive with a defect that is ascertainable through inspection, whether they inspect the car or not, they will be liable for damage caused by that defect."

Notice that the above phrasing of the holding is not "if a driver drives with a bald tire he is responsible for the damage he causes if he tries to pass another car, swerves and hits the other car." That is too narrow. Similarly, "drivers who drive with faulty cars are negligent" is too broad. *Delair* does not speak to latent defects that are not ascertainable by inspection, such as a hidden broken fan belt or dying battery. You need to strike the right balance between breadth and specificity, and you will get better at it with every brief you write.

## ✦ Sample Brief

Your brief could look something like this:

Delair v. McAdoo (1936)

I.   Facts. D's tire blew out and he crashed into P's car. P sued D, claiming D was negligent for driving with bad tires. Jury found for P, D appealed.

II.  Issue. Is it negligent to drive on bad tires?

III. Reasoning.

Rules:
— People should know that when a tire is worn out it's dangerous to drive.
— We must assume that drivers do know that.
— People can't escape liability for the damage bad tires cause just by claiming they weren't aware the tires were bad.

Policy:
— With so many cars on the road we need to hold drivers to a standard of care that will promote safety.
— Because the danger is so great, we need a rule that requires people to inspect their cars and charges them with responsibility for the defects an inspection would reveal.

IV.  Holding. Drivers have a duty to keep their cars safe, and if they drive with a defect that is ascertainable by inspection, whether they inspect their car or not they will be liable for damage caused by that defect.

That's it. That's your brief. If yours is longer, fine. Over time you will hone your skills and cut out more and more dicta. The important part is that you've learned that cases have four distinct elements, the most important of which is the holding. The last thing to note is that sometimes cases will have more than one issue, and if that is the case, your brief necessarily will be longer. Just work through the case exactly the same way, by reading, synthesizing and stating the elements in your own words. The more you practice, the better you'll become.

## ✦ Dicta Column

Briefing is a big responsibility, one you will have to face almost every day of the semester. Take heart knowing that all your work will pay off. Briefing cases will prepare you to be called on in class, to make outlines and to study for your exams. Because it is so important, briefing worries many students.

There are, however, a few things you do not need to worry about as you brief your cases:

✦ *That your classmates write down more than you do.* If you learned anything in this chapter, it should be that "less is more." Although it would seem that the more you write, the more you got out of a case, the opposite is actually true. Unless the case itself is unnaturally long (as some Supreme Court opinions can be), a long brief shows only one thing—that the student didn't take the time to think about the material and decide what's really important. Instead, he just threw everything in, dicta and all. That's not a brief—that's recopying the case.

✦ *Finding elements in a case that don't seem to belong.* The cases that appear in your casebook are edited versions of the actual cases. Because cases are long and wordy and contain issues that touch on different areas of the law, casebook editors cut out a good portion of most cases. They do this to cut the case down so that it relates to only one area of the law and addresses only the specific issue and rule that the casebook editor wants you to learn. Editing is a delicate process, however, and often the cases in your casebook will contain references or facts relating to issues the editor attempted to cut out. Keep this in mind as you read. You will often run across issues or facts that seem completely unrelated to the issue the case is focusing on. Do not spend too much time fighting these facts to make them fit into your brief. Just trust your instincts and leave them out.

✦ *Getting things wrong in your brief.* As you begin briefing, there will be more than a few days when you'll do your brief, go to class the next day and discover from class discussion that some elements of your brief are wrong. Don't worry about it—it happens to everyone. Everyone gets the issue, holding, reasoning and even facts wrong, more than once in a while. This is a learning process. Give yourself time. So if you find parts of your brief are wrong, just cross them out and write in the correct information.

# CHAPTER THREE

# ✦ Learning from Socratic Class Discussion

As you have already noticed, law school classes are very different from college classes. In college, professors taught you a class through lectures. You took notes on what your professor said, and your professor gave you answers when you raised your hand and asked a question. Law school classes, on the other hand, are almost exactly the opposite. Rarely do law school professors lecture. And instead of you asking questions and your professors answering them, professors are the ones asking the questions and students are the ones answering them. Law school professors "call on" students and ask them to answer question after question after question. The students answer the best they can, and law school professors rarely comment on whether the given answers are right or wrong.

This is called Socratic discussion, derived from the teaching method of the Greek philosopher Socrates. The theory is that by asking a series of questions, the teacher forces the student to think through the problem and discover the answer on his or her own. Almost every law professor follows this teaching method, to some extent. On one end of the spectrum are the professors who adhere stringently to the Socratic Method. These professors conduct very formal, "Paper Chase"–like classes, calling students "Mr." or "Ms." and requiring them to stand up to answer questions. If the student performs badly, a strict professor may give the student a verbal thrashing and make her look like an idiot in front of her classmates. Some professors kick students out of class if they haven't done the assigned reading. Others refuse to let students in the door if they are late to class. One professor we know made it a point to reduce at least one student to tears on the first day of class every semester. Why? The age-old answer: Because he could.

On the other end of the spectrum are the professors who reject the strict formality of the Socratic Method and conduct kinder, less anxiety-producing classes. Your professors will fall on different points of the spectrum, and you will have to adjust to their different teaching methods.

The one thing you can expect from all professors is some form of Socratic discussion, where questions beget questions, not answers.

There are four problems that first years face as they first encounter Socratic class discussion:

I.    How to take notes
II.   What to do when a classmate gets called on
III.  What to do when you get called on
IV.   Whether to participate in a study group

This chapter will teach you to tackle all four problems.


# I. Taking Notes

It can be difficult to take notes from Socratic discussion. When the professor is the one asking the questions and a student is the one providing the answers, a problem arises: How do you know what to write down? Professors rarely comment on whether a student's answers are good or bad, and you never know what the professor considers to be a good answer. So how do you know what to write down in your notes?

Most law students answer this question by writing down absolutely everything that is said in class. That's not the right approach, for three reasons. First, if you are madly scribbling notes, you don't have time to actually listen to what's going on. Second, a lot of what is said in class is not important, and you're wasting your time writing it down. Finally, when you go back to read your notes when you start outlining, you'll have to sift through an enormous pile of notes to find the few kernels of worthwhile information.

To take good notes, you need to be active. You must think actively, listen actively and make active, reasoned decisions about what you think is worth writing down and what is not. Really listen to what's going on in class, what issues are being discussed and where your professor guides the conversation. This means that you will listen for stretches of time without taking notes. When you're ready to write, summarize in your own words the discussion that you've been listening to. Of course, if at any time something strikes you as important or helps you understand a concept better, write it down. Above all, remember that it's not the quantity of notes that matters, it's the quality. Here are some guidelines to help you take the best quality notes you can:

✦ *Be organized.* The more organized you are with your notes, the easier it will be to go through your notes later as you start to outline. Loose-leaf paper and three-ring binders are a good way to force yourself to be organized. Buy a binder for each class. Take notes on looseleaf paper, adding pages to your binders as the semester goes along. This way, you can always keep your notes in chronological order, even if you miss a day and have to get someone else's notes or if you lend a day's notes to a friend to copy.

✦ *Be consistent.* Each day in class, take out a clean sheet of paper. Date it at the top. When your professor announces the name of the case you will be discussing, write it down at the top of the page and underline it. This way you will never find yourself wondering where a page of notes came from, even if it gets separated from the rest of your class notes. Binders also allow you to weave in your case briefs into your class notes. As you do your briefs, put them into your binder. Then in class, you will have your brief in front of you as the professor discusses the case. Your brief will help you remember the case and will help you answer the professor's questions if you get called on.

✦ *Listen actively.* Remember, law school is not the place to scribble down notes as fast as you can in an attempt to write down every single thing the professor and students say. This may look like a conscientious way to take notes, but it's actually the lazy way. When you concentrate on writing down absolutely everything, you go on auto-pilot and do not even think about what you are writing. You need to write down only what's important, and deciding what's important requires you to think.

✦ *Ask questions.* Professors often gloss over areas that are not clear to most people. If you don't understand something, raise your hand and ask your professor to explain.

✦ *If your professor does lecture, pay attention.* Rare as it may be, your professor will sometimes lecture on a particular case or area of the law. If this happens, it is because the case is a seminal one, one that you need to learn and understand, one that will probably show up on the final exam. When this happens, your notes can be as copious as you think necessary.

## II. When a Classmate Gets Called On

When one of your classmates gets called on, you need to be very selective about what you choose to write in your notes. Even if the student seems bright or speaks confidently, a student is a student and there's a good possibility that what she says is simply wrong. So as your classmate answers questions, spend time making decisions whether to write down her ideas or not. Evaluate the merits in your own mind. If you think one of the answers is particularly good or compelling, by all means write it in your notes. But for the most part, be selective and realize that many of your classmate's thoughts aren't worth writing down.

At first, this might be difficult. Law school is a serious place; every person in your class is bright and accomplished. As a result, many first years feel intimidated by their classmates and give them more credit than they are actually due. You need to remember that you are bright and accomplished as well, and you can hold your own with any of your classmates.

## III. When You Get Called On

As much as you may try to avoid it, you will get called on at some point during the semester. When you do, your professor will expect you to give a brief recitation of the facts, issue, reasoning and holding of the case you are discussing. If you're organized and have your case brief in front of you, this will not be a problem, no matter how nervous you are. Try to look up at your professor as much as possible, however, or she might think you haven't done the reading and are searching the text of your casebook for answers. After a basic discussion of the case, your professor will vary the facts and ask you to explain how and why you think the hypothetical she posed would be decided. As in the reasoning sections in the cases you read, you will have to give your professor reasons why you think the varied facts would produce a certain outcome. Be prepared to explain your position and defend it if your professor questions it, which she very likely will. Remember as you answer that there are no right or wrong answers—the only thing that matters is how well you can adjust your thinking to different fact patterns and defend your position regarding each of them.

In the best-case scenario, you will have reasonable, legitimate answers to your professor's questions and won't be too nervous to say them. A worst-case scenario is the day you get called on when you haven't done the reading. These can be bad days, depending on how unglued your professor becomes upon learning that you are unprepared. If this happens, the best plan of action is usually to just admit it. You've probably seen other students in your class try to weasel through the professor's questions by pretending they've done the reading, and it's not a pretty sight. If you try to act prepared when you're not, it opens the door for your professor to make you look like a complete idiot in front of the class. A far better plan is to just admit that you're unprepared, apologize and agree to be prepared for the next class. If your professor is on the tyrant end of the professor spectrum, you may get a verbal dressing-down, but at least you won't have to sit through a series of questions that you have no idea how to answer.

If you want to reduce the amount you get called on, try the following tips: Get to class on time, sit in the middle rows, don't chat or pass notes to your neighbor and don't make too much eye contact with the professor. Professors tend to call on the students who stand out, whether it's because they raise their hands a lot, wear Hawaiian shirts, or chew gum and blow bubbles. If you don't want to get called on, making an effort to blend into the fabric of the class will help disguise you. Don't worry if you never say anything remotely intelligent (or anything at all, for that matter) in class, because your performance in class has absolutely nothing to do with your final grade.

# IV. Study Groups

The first year is a nerve-wracking time, and many students try to calm their nerves by joining a study group. Suffering with others seems less painful than suffering alone.

A study group may be comforting, but the truth is that unless you find a particularly bright and hardworking study group, you may find yourself wasting a lot of time. People in groups chat. It takes a group longer to accomplish anything than it takes a person alone. And, every person in the group has a different level of proficiency in the subject.

Because of this, many students who do well choose to forego study groups. If you do decide to join a study group, however, keep in mind the following:

+ *Set specific goals for every meeting.* Once you have accomplished the goal, you are free either to leave or to socialize, but not until then.
+ *If you find at any point that the group isn't working for you, leave.* If you think you're wasting time now, chances are you're going to waste time the whole semester. Cut your losses and move on.
+ *Never study for exams with a group.* You will take your exams alone, not with the members of your study group. When the end of the semester rolls around, it's time to disband the group and go it alone, no matter what.

## ✦ Dicta Column

In no other area of law school are there more things that seem worrisome but really aren't than those involving class. Class is anxiety-producing for many reasons. There's always the potential for being called on. The material you discuss is intellectually challenging, and unfortunately Socratic discussion does not lend itself to clear-cut answers. To make matters worse, many professors consciously try to be intimidating and trade on your fear to cause you anxiety. While all of this is unavoidable, you can avoid unnecessary anxiety by remembering not to worry about the following:

✦ *The guy/girl in your class who knows everything.* In every class at every law school, there is the student who raises her hand in class every day and acts like she knows everything. She might brag that she read the entire casebook the summer before law school began. Often she wears a suit to class and perhaps even carries a briefcase, for no apparent reason other than to look important.

Do not fear this person. She may sound smart to you, and perhaps she is a bright woman. But just as likely, she's not. In fact, quite often the students who finish at the very top of the class are people who never volunteered a word in class during the entire semester.

Everybody has a different way of coping with the stress of law school, and with class in particular. Some people's defense mechanism of choice is being a know-it-all. Just remember that people who talk a lot don't always have something to say. And just because they talk a lot does not by any means indicate that they will do better than you on the final exam.

✦ *Getting yelled at in class.* It's awful to be verbally abused by a professor, especially in front of your peers. It's embarrassing, sometimes even humiliating. You feel like the professor hates you and that everyone in the class thinks you're stupid.

The only thing guaranteed to get rid of the pain of getting yelled at in class is this: "anonymous grading." No matter how angry your professor gets, no matter how scathing her words, and no matter how much you think she hates you, it can never hurt your grades. When it comes to the final exam, you are just a number. Your professor doesn't know you from the man who sits next to you, and she doesn't know him from the woman who wears a suit and talks in class every day. You will be graded solely on the merits of your exam, and the grade on your exam is the only grade you will receive for the entire semester of class. Law school doesn't have many pluses, but anonymous grading is one of them. Your professor's scathing words are just that—words. They can hurt your feelings but they cannot hurt your grades. So if you get yelled at, forget it and move on, because there's nothing you can do about it. If you stop going to class you'll only hurt yourself. If you worry that the rest of the class is laughing at you or thinks you're stupid, you're wasting your time. You have to toughen up. Just remember the words "anonymous grading" and commit yourself to acing your final exam. There's nothing more satisfying than showing the professor who hates you the "A" she gave you on your final exam.

✦ *That you never understand what's going on in class*. This is more common than you think. Socratic discussion is confusing. It causes first years enormous anxiety because they cling to the memory of college, when class meant answers and illumination and real discussion of the material you studied.

Forget college. Law school classes are the opposite of college classes. Your professors purposely muddy the waters. They want to confuse you under the theory that it is good for you because it makes you think. You are supposed to be confused. It's painful, but that's just the way it is. Again, the advice here is that you shouldn't worry about it too much. Most students find that it is not until they sit down to outline the class that a light bulb snaps on in their heads and all of a sudden, things fall into place. After a semester of confusing and aggravating classes, they finally begin to recognize and distinguish issues from rules and facts from dicta. So hang in there. Make a real effort to understand, but when you find that you don't understand, just let it go. Take heart knowing that later in the semester, the light bulb will snap on in your head and you'll finally be able to see what's going on.

✦ *Recopying your notes*. Many first years think that it will help them to recopy their class notes after class. Some even take their class notes home and re-type them every night. Do not do this. While it looks like a conscientious and industrious thing to do, it's actually a waste of time. As you have learned in this chapter, class notes are hit-or-miss to begin with. You write down too much because you're not sure what's important and what isn't. A lot of extraneous, unhelpful information sneaks in there, and you should not waste your time learning it. Certainly you should not waste your time recopying that extraneous information.

Moreover, even when your notes do contain valuable information, recopying is not a thinking-person's activity; it is busy work. Law students are notorious for creating busy work for themselves. They create busy work because, consciously or subconsciously, they are trying to avoid thinking. Law students would rather do anything in the world than think. But thinking is the single most important thing you can do in law school. If you really feel the need to re-hash the day's class, try this exercise: Stare at a wall and try to figure out what really happened in class, what the professor was trying to teach you, and why she was trying to teach you that particular idea. Find the kernel of knowledge that the muddy waters of class discussion obscured, then write it down in no more than three sentences. Staring at a wall and thinking deeply about class is a thousand times more difficult, and more beneficial, than recopying your notes like an automaton.

CHAPTER FOUR
# ✦ Navigating the *Bluebook* of Legal Citation

One of the books you were required to buy at the beginning of the semester but probably haven't opened yet is the *Bluebook*. Because you will have to use this book when you write your first memorandum for legal research and writing class, it would be wise for you to know something about the *Bluebook* before you get that assignment. This chapter will teach you what you need to know.

First, what is the *Bluebook*? The *Bluebook* is exactly what it calls itself—"a uniform system of citation." The *Bluebook*'s citation forms are different from the citation forms you used in your college research papers, where you cited sources using footnotes and endnotes. If you were like most students, you didn't concern yourself too much with the form you used for those footnotes and endnotes. And as long as you kept the footnotes relatively consistent and free of typos, college professors didn't care too much whether the form was correct.

Law professors care. They care enormously. Citation form in legal documents is a rigid, serious and delicate business, one that law students, law professors and especially the staff of Law Reviews take very much to heart. The *Bluebook*, all 350-odd pages of it, contains nothing but citation forms. That's how serious lawyers are about citation. And the *Bluebook*, remarkable book that it is, does little to help you through its sometimes treacherous waters; if the editors have the choice either to oversimplify or overcomplicate, they choose the latter every time. The *Bluebook* is a point of frustration for most law students, but this chapter will simplify and clarify the *Bluebook* and teach you the rules you need to learn.

Before we begin, open up your *Bluebook* and turn to the Index. Pretty amazing, isn't it? If you need to cite auditing standards, Canon Law, colloquia in periodicals, Swiss cantons, the Institutes of Gaius, phrases of location, pleadings in World Court cases, United Nations plenary materials or the sources of law for the Yukon Territory, the *Bluebook* can show you

how. The Index shows you where in the *Bluebook* you can find out how
to cite anything and everything under the sun.

Luckily for you, however, there is little chance that you will have to cite
any of those materials in your first-year legal writing assignments. If you join
the Law Review staff your second year, you will become intimately
acquainted with more citation forms than you'll care to know, but for now,
you need only familiarize yourself with the cite forms you will be required
to use in your first-year legal writing assignments. Although the *Bluebook*
contains thousands of rules of citation, you only need to learn five. They
are:

I.    How to Cite Cases
II.   How to Cite Law Reviews
III.  How to Cite Magazines and Newspapers
IV.   How to Cite Books
V.    How to Cite Codified Law

You can worry about the other thousands of rules of citation later. For
now, you only need to learn five rules, but you need to learn them well.
There is no margin for error in legal citation. You need to be exact,
fastidious and careful. The *Bluebook* contains many traps for the unwary,
and the way to avoid those traps is to follow the rules, and follow them to
the letter. If the *Bluebook* says there should be a space between the "S."
and "Ct." in the abbreviation for the *Supreme Court Reporter*, you'd
better leave a space or your citation is wrong. Similarly, if the *Bluebook*
says something should be underlined, underline it. If the *Bluebook* says the
comma after a case name should not be underlined, do not underline it.
Although these rules seem overwhelming (and a little idiotic) at first, with
practice they will become second nature to you.

As we start our journey through the *Bluebook*, remember that you are
only concerned with citation form for legal memoranda (as opposed to
citation form for law review footnotes) because that is what you will be
assigned to write. The *Bluebook* differentiates between citation form for
these two different writings. Citation form for legal memoranda is
formulated to use the keys you find on a typewriter: upper and lower case
letters, numbers and the underline key. Law review footnotes incorporate
more sophisticated typeface such as italics and large and small capital
letters. Even though most people now use computers and word processors
that offer these more sophisticated printing options, do not use them on
your legal memoranda. You must follow the *Bluebook*'s rules and pretend
your computer is a typewriter.

All five of the rules you are about to learn are listed in one section of
the *Bluebook*. Open your *Bluebook* to the last page, and inside the back

cover you will find a section called "Quick Reference: Court Documents and Legal Memoranda." This is the most helpful section of the book, one you will turn to over and over again as you write legal documents. Not only does this section show you examples of every rule you need to know for your first-year legal writing, it also tells you where you can find the full rules in the text of the *Bluebook*. We will use the examples in the Quick Reference to illustrate the rules you need to learn, so keep that section in front of you as you read this chapter.

# I. How to Cite Cases

The first examples listed in the Quick Reference are how to cite reported cases. As Quick Reference tells you, the full rule for citing reported cases is found in rule 10 of the *Bluebook*. The Quick Reference also provides you with two examples of case citation:

Jackson v. Metropolitan Edison Co., 348 F. Supp. 954, 956–58 (M.D. Pa. 1972), aff'd, 483 F.2d 754 (3d Cir. 1973), aff'd, 419 U.S. 345 (1974).

Herrick v. Lindley, 59 Ohio St. 2d 22, 23–25, 391 N.E. 2d 729, 731 (1979).

Why are there two examples rather than one? Because the first example, *Jackson*, is a federal case and the second, *Herrick*, is a state case. Citation forms for federal and state cases are a bit different, although only slightly, and the rules for citing cases that you will learn in this section apply to both state and federal cases, unless otherwise indicated.

Citation form for all cases contains the following four elements: the case name, the reporter, the page number or numbers, and the parenthetical. In some instances, you must also include a fifth element, something called "subsequent history." When a case citation has these four or five elements, the citation is called a "full cite." Later in this section you will learn the "short form" of citation that you use only after you have provided a full citation for every case you cite. We'll take each element of the full cite in turn, using the examples of *Jackson* and *Herrick* above.

## A. The Case Name

In every case citation, the case name is underlined. The names of the parties are separated with a "v.", not "vs." As in all titles, the words that make up case names are capitalized, except for prepositions, conjunctions and articles. Look at the *Jackson* example and you will see how capitalization works. You also will see in the *Jackson* example that the word "Company" is abbreviated to "Co." The *Bluebook* requires you to abbreviate some words in case names. Table T.6 provides a list of all the words you must abbreviate when you cite cases. If one of the words in the case name you want to cite appears on the list in Table T.6, you must abbreviate that word. Remember, however, that you never abbreviate the first word of either party. The final thing to notice about case names is that there is always a comma after the name of the case, and that the comma is not underlined.

## B. The Reporter

The next part of case citation indicates where the case appears in its reporter. You know what reporters are, both official and unofficial, from Chapter One. You also know what the numbers before and after the reporter mean: The volume number comes before the reporter and the first page of the case comes after.

The reporter element is the first of the three instances where cite form for state and federal cases differs. If you look closely at the *Jackson* and *Herrick* examples, you will see that in *Herrick*, there is reference made to two reporters: the state (Ohio) and the regional (N.E.2d), whereas in the *Jackson* example, there is a reference only to F. Supp. One difference between citing state and federal cases is that when you cite state cases, you must refer both to the state and regional reporter. For federal cases, you need only cite to the official reporter.

### 1. Federal Cases

You already know that the *Federal Reporter* is abbreviated as "F.", and that the *Federal Supplement* is abbreviated as "F. Supp." As you see from the *Jackson* example, there is a space between the "F." and "Supp." Currently, federal circuit court decisions are reported in three series of the *Federal Reporter*: "F.", "F.2d", and "F.3d". Federal district court decisions are reported in two series of the *Federal Supplement*: "F. Supp." and "F. Supp. 2d".

### 2. State Cases

State and regional reporters will be less familiar to you than federal reporters for two reasons. First, you read more federal cases than state. Second, there are more reporters to keep track of in the state system. Most of the fifty states have their own state reporters, plus there are seven regional reporters in the state system, whereas the federal system has only the *Federal Reporter* and the *Federal Supplement*. Do not worry about learning the abbreviations for Ohio courts or any other state courts, however. You don't need to learn any of them, because all the information you need is contained in the blue pages near the end of the *Bluebook*. Table T.1 shows you how to cite every state reporter and its corresponding regional reporter after covering citation for federal reporters. Beginning with Alabama courts, the *Bluebook* goes alphabetically through all fifty states and other United States jurisdictions, including Guam and Puerto Rico. Table T.1 is all you need to correctly cite state cases.

## C. Page Numbers

In all full case citations, you must include the page number on which the case begins. In addition, if you are citing the case for a specific proposition (such as the holding) or are taking a direct quote from the case, you also must provide the page number or numbers from which that proposition or quote came. The goal of legal citation is to be as exact as possible. From reading your citation, you want the reader to be able to go to the reporter you cited and flip directly to the precise page on which the cited material appears. So, it is not enough merely to provide the first page on which the case begins; you also must include the specific pages on which your cited material is printed. This is called a "pinpoint cite." The *Jackson* example shows you how to do pinpoint cites. In the *Jackson* example, you will see that after the volume and page of the reporter, there is a comma, then the numbers 956–58. Those numbers are the page numbers on which the specific material cited is found—the pinpoint cite.

If you turn to the *Herrick* example, you will see that pinpoint cites for state cases are a bit more tedious, because you must provide the pinpoint cite for both reporters, the state and the regional. This is the second instance where citation form for state and federal cases differs.

The only other thing you need to know about page numbers is that there is a rule governing how you number pages. Rule 3.3 of the *Bluebook* states that when you refer to multiple pages, you must use a single dash to separate the pages spanned, and you must retain the last two digits of the number but drop other repetitive digits. For example, 956–958 is not correct. The "9" is a repetitive digit, so it is dropped, leaving the correct 956–58.

## D. The Parenthetical

The final element of full case citations is the parenthetical. Look again at the *Jackson* and *Herrick* examples to see what is included in the parenthetical in state and federal cases.

### 1. State Cases

The *Herrick* cite contains only the date of the case in the parenthetical, because that is all we need to know. The other elements of the cite already provided all the other information we could want to know about *Herrick*. The case was reported in the *Ohio State Reports* (abbreviated as "Ohio St."), which informs the reader that the case was decided by the Ohio Supreme Court (Table T.1), and we know where we can find the case in the state and regional reporters. All that is left is the date the case was decided, and that is what you put in the parenthetical.

### 2. United States Supreme Court Cases

Similarly, when you cite cases decided by the United States Supreme Court, all you need to put in the parenthetical is the date the Court decided the case. Both the official reporter, the *United States Reports* (abbreviated "U.S.") and the unofficial reporter, the *Supreme Court Reporter* (abbreviated "S. Ct.") report cases from only one court: the United States Supreme Court. So, from a cite like <u>Roe v. Wade</u>, 391 U.S. 486 (1973), we know everything we need to know—the court that decided the case, where it is reported and when it was decided.

### 3. Federal Court Cases

The parenthetical in federal cases is the third and final instance where citing state and federal cases differs. The *Jackson* example shows you that when citing federal cases, the parenthetical requires a bit more information than state case citation. Because there are only two main federal reporters, the *Federal Reporter* and the *Federal Supplement*, you cannot tell from the reporter element of the cite where the case came from. So, you have to use the parenthetical element of the cite to show exactly what court issued the opinion (which is also true of state cases in some, but not all, instances).

The *Jackson* example shows you what to put in the parenthetical when you are citing a federal *district court case*. We see from the reporter element of the cite that the case is a federal district court case, because it is reported in the *Federal Supplement*. But which district court decided the case? In the parenthetical, we see that the case came from "M.D. Pa.", which means the middle district of Pennsylvania. How do we know that? Because "Pa." is the generally accepted abbreviation for Pennsylvania, and because "M.D." means "middle district." District courts differentiate themselves by location, and you must memorize seven abbreviations right now: D., M.D., N.D., S.D., E.D., C.D. and W.D., which stand for District, Middle District, Northern District, Southern District, Eastern District, Central District and Western District.

When citing federal *appellate court cases* you must indicate which circuit decided the case in the parenthetical. As you know from Chapter One, there are eleven circuits in the United States, plus the District of Columbia Circuit and the Federal Circuit. Circuit is abbreviated as "Cir.", and the numbers of the circuits are abbreviated as follows: 1st, 2d, 3d, 4th, 5th, 6th, 7th, 8th, 9th, 10th, 11th, D.C. and Fed. For example, a case from the Fifth Circuit is cited as follows: <u>United States v. Palmer</u>, 31 F.3d 259 (5th Cir. 1994).

## E. Subsequent History

"Subsequent history" is an odd term, but what it means is "what happened to the case after it was decided by the court whose opinion you are citing." "Subsequent activity" might be more correct, but it's called subsequent history, so get used to it. In Chapter Six's lesson on legal writing on legal research you will learn the rules of when you must include subsequent history in your case citations. For now, you only need to learn how to cite subsequent history should you need to.

If you look at the *Jackson* example again, you will notice that the citation doesn't end with a citation to the federal district court in Pennsylvania. Instead, there is the word "<u>aff'd</u>" after the first parenthetical. This is the abbreviation for "affirmed," and it is always underlined. All the abbreviations you will need to use to explain subsequent history are included in Table T.9 of the *Bluebook*.

The example shows us that the *Jackson* case went to the Third Circuit and then to the United States Supreme Court. Notice that you cite each court's decision exactly the same way you would in a normal full citation, just without repeating the case name. Each full cite is separated by commas, and no pinpoint cites are necessary.

## F. Short Form Citation Forms

You're almost finished with case citation. The final thing you need to learn is how to cite cases using a short form. The rule is that once you have cited a source in your document using the full cite, you thereafter cite to that case using one of the following two shortened citation forms: (1) Id., or (2) short form citation.

### 1. Id.

Using id. is easy. "Id." is capitalized when it is the first word in the cite and is always underlined, including the period. Always use ibid, abbreviated as id., if you cite the same case two or more times in a row. For example, if you wanted to cite *Jackson* twice in a row in your memo, use a full cite the first time you cite from it. After that, you would use id. If the material you wished to cite were on page 960 of *Jackson* rather than on the pages in the full cite, you would write "Id. at 960." Use id. to cite *Jackson* until you cite another source. Then, if you wish to cite *Jackson* again, use one of the short forms below.

### 2. Short Form Citation

Short form citation is almost as easy as id. The rule is that after you have given a full cite for the case once in your document, you use short form to cite to it thereafter. The *Bluebook* gives you two different options for short form citing: You may use either one of the parties' names or both, followed by a shortened form of the reporter element. You could cite *Jackson* either of the two following ways:

Jackson, 348 F. Supp. at 960.

Jackson v. Metropolitan Edison Co., 348 F. Supp. at 960.

Notice that you do not have to provide the first page on which the case appears, the parenthetical with the court that decided the case, or the date the case was decided. Instead, you simply use the word "at" to indicate where your quoted material appears. You may use either of the above short forms, but the first is more common, shorter, and easier. If you choose to use the first method, the rule is to use the first party's name as the short form name, unless the first party's name is something very common, such as "United States." Every federal criminal case has United States as its first party's name, so using it in the short form does nothing to help distinguish it from any other case. The correct thing to do in such circumstances is to use the second name in the case name in your short form citation.

## II. How to Cite Law Reviews

You will no doubt be pleased to know that citing law reviews is much simpler than citing cases. There are only two citation forms you need to learn: full and short. The rules for both forms are rigid and without exception.

Turn to the back of your *Bluebook*. At the top of the back inside cover you will find an example of how to cite a law review article. The *Bluebook* overcomplicates this by calling the journal not a law review but a "consecutively paginated journal." That just means that every time a new volume of the journal begins, it begins on page one, and the numbers continue to run throughout the issues in that volume until a new volume begins. All law reviews work that way.

### A. Full Citation Form

The example of a full cite for law reviews in the Quick Reference reads:

> Patricia J. Williams, Alchemical Notes: Reconstructed Ideals from Deconstructed Rights, 22 Harv. C.R.-C.L. L. Rev. 401, 407 (1987).

This is a full citation. It consists of four elements: the name of the author, the title of the article, the journal of publication and date it was published. We'll take each one in turn.

#### 1. Author's Name

Notice that the name of the author is written in full, first name first and last name last, followed by a comma.

#### 2. Title

The title of the article is always underlined. The title is followed by a comma which is never underlined. Unlike the cite form for case names, do not abbreviate words in the titles of law review articles.

#### 3. Journal

This part looks difficult, but it's not. For once, the *Bluebook* makes things very easy on you and spoon feeds you what you need to know. Turn to Table T.13 of your *Bluebook*, and there you will find every journal you could ever want to cite and the correct way to abbreviate it. Remember that although the abbreviations appear in the *Bluebook* in large and small capital letters, you must follow the rules for legal memoranda, not law review footnotes, so you will use roman text.

Just as in case citations, the volume of the periodical comes before the abbreviated name and the page the article begins on comes after. If you are citing a specific page or pages, write the pinpoint cite just as you do with cases. Include the pages the material spans, separated by a single dash, keeping the last two numbers and dropping any repetitious numbers.

### 4. Date

The year the article was published goes in the parenthetical, followed by a period.

## B. Short Citation Forms

### 1. Id.

Just as you do with cases, you must use id. if you cite the same article two or more times in a row. The first time you cite a law review, give a full cite, and after that use id. until you cite another source.

### 2. Supra

If you give the full cite of a law review and then later in your document want to cite it again, you must use supra, which means "before." For example, the following is how you would use a short form citation to cite the above example at page 405:

Williams, supra, at 405.

That's all there is to citing law review articles.

## III. How to Cite Magazines and Newspapers

Citing magazines and newspapers is similar to citing law review articles, only easier. Turn to the Quick Reference for examples of how it's done.

## A. Magazines

In keeping with its tendency to overcomplicate, the *Bluebook* calls magazines "nonconsecutively paginated journals." This, of course, means journals that begin every issue on page one (in other words, magazines). The full text of how to cite "nonconsecutively paginated journals," or magazines, can be found in rule 16.3.

The example of a full magazine citation provided by the Quick Reference is:

Lynn Hirschberg, <u>The Misfit</u>, Vanity Fair, Apr. 1991, at 158.

Full cites require the author's name, the title of the article (underlined), the name of the magazine, the date and the page on which the cited material appears. Do not abbreviate words in the titles of magazine articles. Notice too that the page number is prefaced by "at."

Short form citation of magazine articles is the same as that for law review articles.

## B. Newspapers

Like magazines, newspapers are very easy to cite. The examples given in the Quick Reference are:

Andrew Rosenthal, <u>White House Tutors Kremlin in How a Presidency Works</u>, N.Y. Times, June 15, 1990, at A1, A7.

<u>Cop Shoots Tire, Halts Stolen Car</u>, S.F. Chron., Oct. 10, 1975, at 43.

The first example shows how to cite an article written by a particular reporter. Like magazine citation, you provide the name of the author, the title (underlined), the newspaper, the date and the page. This story appears on the front page, A1, and a later page, A7. The second example shows you how to cite an article without a byline. Just provide the title, the newspaper, the date and the page.

Short form citation for newspapers works exactly the same as law reviews and magazines. Use <u>id.</u> when appropriate.

# IV. How to Cite Books

There are three types of books you will cite in your legal writing class: single-edition books, multiple-edition books and multi-volume books. While this seems complicated, it's really not. Like magazines, books are easy to cite; you just need to determine which of the three types of books you want to cite and then follow the rules. The Quick Reference provides examples of how to cite all three types of books, and rule 15 of the *Bluebook* contains the full text of the rule. We'll take each type of book in turn.

## A. Single-Edition Books

The easiest cite form of all is the single-edition book. The example provided by the Quick Reference is:

Deborah L. Rhode, <u>Justice and Gender</u> 56 (1989).

Pretty simple. Just provide the full name of the author, the title (underlined), the page on which the cited material appears and the year. Notice there is no "at" before the page number. That's all there is to it.

Short form citation is exactly the same as that for law reviews, magazines and newspapers. Use <u>id.</u> when appropriate.

## B. Multi-Edition Books

Citing multi-edition books is only slightly more complicated than single-edition books. How do you know when a book has more than one edition? Turn to the inside cover, where the information about copyright and reprinting is located. There you see whether there is more than one edition of the book.

The example provided in the Quick Reference, Charles Dickens's *Bleak House*, is obviously a book with multiple editions:

Charles Dickens, <u>Bleak House</u> 49–55 (Norman Page ed., Penguin Books 1971) (1853).

Remember, the point of all legal citation is to enable the reader to go to the book you used and find your cited material right away. So, you want to indicate the particular edition of the multiple-edition book that you used, and you do that in the same place you indicate a court when citing cases: in the parenthetical.

Again, the short form citation of books is exactly like that for law review articles and magazines, newspapers and single-edition books. Use id. when appropriate.

## C. Multi-Volume Works

Some of the books you will cite are part of multi-volume sets. The example in the Quick Reference is:

> 21 Charles A. Wright & Kenneth A. Graham, Jr., Federal Practice and Procedure § 5023 (1977).

Notice that the volume number goes before the authors' names, not before the title as it does with cases and law review articles. Notice also that multiple authors are linked with an ampersand, not the word "and." There is no comma after the title, and there is a space between the section symbol and the section number. Notice also that there is no page number. That is because almost all of the multi-volume books on legal subjects are separated into sections, and when they are, you cite to the section number rather than the page number. If a multi-volume set is not separated into sections, then you would cite to the page number.

If this multi-volume book were not the first edition, you would have to indicate that too, because again, the point of legal citation is to tell the reader exactly where they can find the material you cited. Like case citations and citation of multi-edition books, that extra information goes in the parenthetical. So if the book cited above were the third edition, you would cite it as follows:

> 21 Charles A. Wright & Kenneth A. Graham, Jr., Federal Practice and Procedure § 5023 (3d ed. 1977).

The short form citation for multi-volume works is like the short form citation of magazines, law review articles at other books. Use id. when appropriate. The short form of the example above is:

> Wright & Graham, supra, at § 5023.

The only time the short form would be different is if you cited to more than one volume of this book in your document. Say for example you cited to both volume 21 and volume 10 of this book in your document. You would need to distinguish which volume your cite referred to, volume 10 or volume 21. So, your short forms for this multi-volume work would look like this:

10 Wright & Graham, <u>supra</u>, at § 2103.

21 Wright & Graham, <u>supra</u>, at § 5203.

# V. How to Cite Codified Law

The last rule you need to know is how to cite the law, which is collected or "codified" in the code books. There are hundreds of statutes, ordinances and regulations, both federal and state. We call all these things laws, and all these laws, from federal civil rights laws to the local ordinances that restrict where you can park your car in your hometown, are all printed in a code book somewhere.

While you do need to appreciate the sheer number and variety of laws, you do not need to know how to cite very many of them. Your professors expect you to teach yourself how to do legal research (which you will learn in Chapter Five), but they do not want you to spend so much time wading through the code books that you don't have any time to actually write your memo. Chances are, you will only need to cite two kinds of law in your first-year writing class: constitutions and statutes. Here's how.

## A. Constitutions

All state constitutions and the United States Constitution are cited the same way. An example of how to cite constitutions is provided in the Quick Reference, and the full rule is found in rule 11 of the *Bluebook*. The example in the Quick Reference is:

N.M. Const. art. IV, § 7.

This is a cite to article four, section seven of the New Mexico constitution. The state abbreviation always comes first, as does "U.S." when you are citing the United States Constitution. Constitution is always abbreviated "Const." The article comes next, and the number of the article is in roman numerals. The section is marked with a section sign, and the number of the section is in Arabic numerals. The clause, if there is one, is abbreviated "cl." and the number of the clause is in Arabic numerals. For example:

U.S. Const. art I, § 9, cl. 2.

Articles, sections, and clauses are separated by commas. The abbreviations for amendments and preambles are listed in rule 11 of the *Bluebook*. The last thing to remember about citing constitutions is that there is no short form citation other than id.

## B. Federal Statutes

Like United States Supreme Court cases, federal statutes are reported both officially and unofficially. Chances are that in your first-year legal writing, you will use the official reporter, the *United States Code*, which is abbreviated U.S.C. Two examples of how to cite the *United States Code* are provided in the Quick Reference, and the full rule is rule 12 of the *Bluebook*. The examples are:

Administrative Procedure Act § 6, 5 U.S.C. § 555 (1994).

22 U.S.C. § 2567 (Supp. I 1983).

Notice that the first example includes the name of the Administrative Procedure Act. Some statutes have names, and others don't. If the statute you want to cite has a name, include it. Otherwise, the second example is how you will cite your statute.

If you are using the official code, you can skip this paragraph and go directly to the Dicta Column at the end of this chapter. If for some reason, however, you have to use the unofficial statutes, here's what you need to know. The most common unofficial code is the *United States Code Annotated*, by West Publishing Company and abbreviated U.S.C.A. Also available is the *United States Code Service*, abbreviated as U.S.C.S., published by Bancroft-Whitney. Cite form for unofficial codes is basically identical to that for official codes. The only difference is that in the parenthetical, you must include the edition and publisher of that code. Here's how it looks:

42 U.S.C.A. § 300a-7 (West Supp. 1991).

## ✦ Dicta Column

The above lessons are all you need to know about the *Bluebook* for now. If you earn a spot on the Law Review or Moot Court, you will have to delve deeper into the *Bluebook* and become much more conversant in its thousands of lessons. For now, however, do not waste your time learning citation forms you have no reason to know. In addition:

✦ *Do not try to learn more than you need to know.* To illustrate this point, take the first rule you learned in this chapter, how to cite cases. You probably noticed in the Quick Reference that underneath the example of how to cite reported cases there were examples of how to cite cases reported in a "service" and how to cite "pending and unreported cases." You'll notice a lot of that going on in the *Bluebook*. The *Bluebook* gives you an enormous amount of information, more information, in fact, than you will ever need to know. Unless you have occasion to cite a pending or unreported case, don't even read that section of the *Bluebook*. Just read the sections that tell you what you need to know and move on. Don't worry about memorizing. Lawyers who have been practicing for years and years don't know all the rules; they still flip through the *Bluebook* to locate citation form.

✦ *Realize that the* Bluebook *is a reference guide.* Unlike your book of Federal Rules of Civil Procedure, you don't have to memorize the *Bluebook*. It's a reference guide; that's all it is. Because it is a reference guide, you don't have to worry about learning how to cite every kind of source. In fact, you don't have to learn any of the cite forms in the *Bluebook* if you don't want to. Memorizing a select few will save you time in the long run, but you do have the option to just look them up over and over again. That's the beauty of the *Bluebook*. All you have to do is use the Index. If you need to know how to cite a source you've never seen before, just look it up. It will answer any citation form question you could ever have.

✦ *Do not worry about citation form on anything other than your legal writing assignments.* Although it's good practice for you to use correct citation form when you write a case citation in your class notes or briefs, it's not necessary. It is also not required on exam answers, so do not waste time on exams using the proper form. Only worry about citation form on the memoranda you write in your legal research and writing class.

CHAPTER FIVE
# ✦ Legal Research

When first years get their first legal research and writing assignment, their natural reaction is to go straight to the library and wander the maze-like shelves of digests, reporters, codes, law reviews, Shepard's Citations, ALRs and so on, searching for what they need to complete the assignment. They don't know what they're looking for and, consequently, they spend a lot of time looking and not much time finding. They get tangled in a confusing web of materials, not knowing where they're going, following the wrong paths, discovering the wrong materials and quite often ending up with the wrong answer.

Needless to say, this is not a wise approach. When you get your first legal research and writing assignment, take half an hour to read this chapter. This chapter will explain the basics:

I.   The goals of legal research
II.  What you are looking for
III. How to find it
IV.  What secondary sources are available

Legal research can be a complicated and delicate process, but once you understand the basics, legal research will go from being a difficult and complicated task to one you will do with confidence and ease.


## I. The Goals of Legal Research

The foundation of all case law in this country is the concept of *stare decisis*, that courts must follow prior precedent. Ideally, your goal in legal research is to find law from your jurisdiction ("controlling" law) that has identical facts (is "on point"). *Stare decisis* requires that such law, law that is controlling and on point, will govern the outcome of your issue.

The first step towards finding this law, no matter what your assignment, is to define your issue. What is it your assignment is asking you to do? What is the dispute to be resolved? To force yourself to narrow the issue, write the issue in as few words as you can, limiting yourself to one sentence.

Once you have defined your issue, you need to gather what information you have to resolve that issue by asking yourself three questions:

✦    What are the relevant and necessary facts?
✦    What are the key words and phrases?
✦    What jurisdiction's laws will govern?

Now that you know what the question is and what information you have to work with, you can start thinking about where to look for the answer.

## II. What You're Looking For

As you know, there are two primary sources of law in the United States: laws (including statutes, regulations, ordinances and other codified legislation, which we refer to here collectively as "statutes") and judicial opinions. Your goal in legal research is to find the statute or judicial opinion(s) that are on point and control your issue. Ideally, you want to find a statute and cases from your jurisdiction that are factually identical or very similar to your issue. If there is no statute (i.e., if the rule of law is derived from the common law) then you want to locate all of the judicial opinions addressing the issue.

It's great when you find what you're looking for. Sometimes, however, things don't work out so simply. There may be no statute. There may be no case from your jurisdiction with even remotely similar facts (let alone identical ones) that addresses your issue. What do you do then?

Then you have to get creative. When there is no controlling law that is on point, your goal changes a little. Whereas your ideal goal is to find the controlling statute and/or judicial opinions that are on point, your goal in this situation is to do the best you can. First, you should look for a case or statute from your jurisdiction with facts that are similar or akin to your facts in some way. You can use this case or statute to argue that this law should apply to your facts and should produce the same result.

Second, you should look outside your jurisdiction for cases that have identical facts. These cases are on point but not controlling, and you will use them to argue that your court should follow the reasoning of the court who

who wrote the opinion. Although *stare decisis* does not require your court to follow the law from another jurisdiction, such cases and statutes are persuasive authority on your court.

# III. How to Find What You're Looking For

This is the most difficult element of legal research for many law students, not just first years. With all the resources available to you in your library to help you locate the law you need, where do you start?

It depends on what you're starting with. Sometimes your legal research assignment will give you a head start with either a case or a statute. Other times, however, you will to start from scratch. The following examples show you step-by-step the approach you should take in each of these situations.

## A. Example #1: You Have a Judicial Opinion

If you are given a judicial opinion to start you on your legal research assignment (we'll call it "Case A"), the first thing to do is read the opinion. Make sure that it is from your jurisdiction (controlling) and that the facts are sufficiently similar (on point). The next thing to do is find out whether Case A is still good law—that is, make sure it has not been modified or overruled by a subsequent judicial opinion or nullified by the legislature. The best way to do this is to use one of the electronic databases, either WESTLAW or LEXIS. Your law school will give you a password and offer you basic training on how to use these databases. Take advantage of these training sessions, because when you know how to use them well, these databases are the best and most efficient methods of conducting legal research once you have located one judicial opinion on point.

To check the status of Case A, log on to one of the databases and go to the service for Shepard's Citations. This service will tell you whether Case A is still good law. It also will identify all the other cases that have cited Case A. In one step you will have determined whether Case A is still good law and found other cases that mention Case A.

The next thing to do is to determine from Case A whether there is a "headnote number" assigned to the specific issue that you want to research. Headnotes are provided by the editors of the case reporter at the beginning of every case to separate the case into different parts. Each headnote is a one-sentence treatment of a single issue or rule of law. Let's say Case A has a particular headnote (we'll call it headnote 4) that is directly on point. You can use that headnote to locate more cases on point in the following ways:

✦   *Use the electronic database.* Both WESTLAW and LEXIS have special services that are essentially abridged and improved versions of Shepard's Citations: KeyCite on WESTLAW and Auto-Cite on LEXIS. In addition to allowing you to view the negative history of your case (subsequent cases that criticize, distinguish or overrule your case) they also provide specific information about headnotes and will tell you whether any subsequent cases have addressed the same issue as your headnote 4.

✦   *Use digests.* In addition to KeyCite or Auto-Cite, you can also use books called "digests" to locate more cases that discuss your headnote 4. Digests collect and catalog cases that discuss the same legal issue. West Publishing Company, for example, publishes digests for the United States Supreme Court, federal courts and for state and regional reporters. These digests are based on the headnotes used by West, and each headnote is identified by a particular West digest topic and key number. Once you know that topic and key number, you can search in the appropriate West digest (the digest for your jurisdiction) to find similar decisions. These decisions may not cite the judicial opinion from which you found headnote 4, but all the cases will discuss the same issue.

Now that you are branching out and are finding other cases that discuss your issue, let's say you find another case, Case B, that is particularly helpful in that it goes into an extended discussion of headnote 4 from Case A. What do you do?

Repeat the process that you followed with Case A. Use Shepard's Citations, KeyCite or Auto-Cite and the appropriate West digest to see whether subsequent cases have discussed Case B and the issues decided in it, using the new headnote number in Case B.

## B. Example #2: You Have a Statute

In this example we'll assume you begin your assignment with a citation to one particular statute. We'll call it Statute 101. How do you determine whether this statute is good law and whether it applies to your issue?

The first place to start is Shepard's Citations. Shepard's Citations will tell you whether Statute 101 has been amended, superseded or repealed.

Shepard's Citations also will list the judicial opinions that have discussed Statute 101.

Why should you care about judicial opinions that have discussed Statute 101? Because a judicial opinion interpreting and applying Statute 101 establishes precedent, and *stare decisis* requires lower courts in the same jurisdiction to follow that interpretation. Further, statutes are only as good as the interpretation they are given by the judiciary. You will find many occasions when you read a statute and the plain language will seem to mean one thing, but judicial interpretation of the statute will dictate a different result. If the judicial decision was rendered by a higher court in the same jurisdiction, the judicial interpretation governs the lower court's interpretation of the statute.

Next, you should look in the annotated version of the code that contains Statute 101. If Statute 101 is a federal statute, it will be found in West Publishing Company's *United States Code Annotated*. If Statute 101 is a state statute, it will be found in that state's annotated code. California statutes are contained in Deering's *Annotated California Code* and West's *Annotated California Codes*. Annotated codes provide a listing of all the judicial opinions that cite the statutes contained in the code, and each of these judicial opinions is discussed in a one- or two-sentence summary.

Once you have located your statute in the code, review the entries that cite your statute until you locate one or more entries that discuss your issue. Pull the case or cases and read them. If they are on point, follow the procedure explained in Example 1 above to find more judicial opinions.

## C. Example #3: You Have No Judicial Opinion, No Statute, and No Clue

In this situation, your professor hands you a legal research and writing assignment and gives you nothing to go on. You're starting from scratch, the way real lawyers do every day. What do you do?

First, don't panic. And don't run out to the library determined to jump in and start hunting around right away. This is inefficient and frustrating. Instead, start at the beginning by defining your issue and answering your three questions: What are the relevant and necessary facts? What are the key words and phrases? What jurisdiction's laws will govern?

With your answers in hand, you can begin your research. The first thing to do is pay a visit to your law library's librarian. Most law school libraries employ at least one librarian who has a law degree as well as a degree in library science. These people know an enormous amount about legal research. They are also an underused resource, because most first years never think to ask them for help. Now that you know better, you can take your issue and the answers to your three questions to your law librarian. Ask him where to begin locating legal authority for your specific problem. In all likelihood, your librarian will be happy to help and will help you construct an efficient and effective search, which will shave hours off your research time.

Another underused resource is your law school's WESTLAW or LEXIS representative. These people are paid to help you do legal research, because they are extremely skilled at it. Take your issue and the three answers to your questions to your representative and get some free assistance with your search.

If for some reason, however, these resources are not available to you, that's fine. You can do it all on your own, and we'll use an example to show you how. Let's say that you have the following information: Defendant, a California resident, made a false and injurious statement in California that Plaintiff, also a California resident, had a venereal disease. Defendant's statement was made during a deposition in an unrelated matter. Defendant admitted that he did not know whether the statement was true or false at the time it was made. Plaintiff sues Defendant in California state court.

That's all you know. But with that, you can define your issue and answer your three questions. The issue is whether Defendant is liable to Plaintiff in tort for making the false statement that plaintiff had a venereal disease. The relevant facts are that Defendant stated during a deposition that Plaintiff had a venereal disease and admitted that he didn't know whether it was true or false. The key words and phrases for this issue are libel, slander, privilege and malice, to name a few. The jurisdiction is obviously California. Now what do you do?

A smart place to start is with a "summary of the law." Almost all states have a treatise or treatises that summarize the law in that state, such as Witkin's *Summary of California Law*. When you know absolutely nothing about an issue, begin your search there. Look through the index for your key words, then read the appropriate sections. Reading this summary of the law will give you a general idea what is going on in a particular area of the law.

Next, go to the appropriate annotated code book for your jurisdiction. In California, Deering's *Annotated California Code* annotates all the statutes enacted in California. In the index, look for your key words, then read the appropriate sections of law governing your issue. This will give you a basic idea of what the law is in this area, and because the code book is annotated, it will lead you to various case citations and synopses. Sort through the case synopses and locate two or three judicial opinions that look promising, then read the opinions to see if they are on point. Through this process, you should find at least one judicial opinion that addresses your issue. With this opinion in hand, go back to Example #1 and proceed with your research.

If this approach doesn't lead you to a judicial opinion, however, don't panic. You have other options. There are several "secondary sources" available to you, such as law reviews, *American Law Reports*, legal encyclopedias and Restatements of the Law. Armed with your key words, you can look in the index of any of these sources to learn more about your issue and be guided in a research direction. Most of these sources offer case citations and statute citations, so you can pull the opinions and statutes referred to, read them, and hopefully find one that is on point. From there, go back and refine your research following the guidelines outlined in Examples #1 and #2.

# IV. What Secondary Sources Are Available

Secondary sources are just what they sound like—secondary. They are a means by which you can find the primary sources you need (judicial opinions and statutes), but they do not carry much legal weight on their own. The only time to cite to a secondary source as legal authority is if you really cannot find anything else to support your position. The secondary sources available to you are:

## A. Encyclopedias

The two main legal encyclopedias are *Corpus Juris Secundum* (the C.J.S.) and *American Jurisprudence 2d* (Am. Jur. 2d). The C.J.S. and Am. Jur. 2d provide a simple look at different areas of the law. Be aware, however, that the entries in these sources are generally not as helpful as the citations listed in the footnotes. Thus, you should use these sources primarily to find case and statute citations, not for the substance of the entries.

## B. Law Reviews

Law reviews are a helpful resource for several reasons. First, law review articles discuss in depth a specific issue or area of the law, and just by reading an article you can learn an enormous amount about its topic. Second, the sources cited in law review articles are exhaustive; authors put a lot of effort into thoroughly researching their topics, and the sources they cite include just about everything you could ever need to know about that particular topic. If you find a law review article that is devoted specifically to your topic, you're in luck. It is sure to be chock-full of cross-references to other law review articles, statutes and judicial opinions that you can use in your research. Remember, however, that while law review articles help your research process enormously, you should rarely use them as authority. You may cite to law review articles to explain a legal concept or define some legal theory, but because law review articles do not hold any legal weight in and of themselves, you should steer clear of relying on a law review article as support for your legal position or conclusion.

The best way to find law review articles on your particular topic is in a publication called the *Index to Legal Periodicals*, which contains an index of most major law reviews. They also can be located on the electronic databases using your key words and phrases.

## C. Restatements of the Law

Restatements of the Law are prepared by the American Law Institute and provide a statement of the general law of the United States. Restatements cover ten areas of law: agency, conflict of laws, contracts, foreign relations law, judgments, property, restitution, security, torts and trusts. Restatements are a series of written rules of law, supplemented by commentary and illustrations of how the laws work. If the Restatement contains a rule of law that is on point for your issue, check the Appendix to find out whether there are published judicial opinions in your jurisdiction that discuss the rule as stated by the Restatement. In addition, you may wish to check a Shepard's publication called *Restatement of the Law Citations*, which provides a list of judicial opinions on the cited topic.

## D. American Law Reports

Unlike West's digest system, which reports all decisions in a particular area of the law, *American Law Reports* (A.L.R.s), report only the most important cases in a particular area of the law. State court decisions from 1966 to the present are reported in the A.L.R.3d and A.L.R.4th. Federal court decisions are reported in the A.L.R. Federal. A.L.R. and A.L.R.2d report both state and federal decisions issued prior to 1966.

To locate cases in the A.L.R. series, use the "Quick Index" for the appropriate A.L.R. series. When you find an entry that deals with your key words and phrases, go to that entry and review the annotations for a case on point. Even if the annotations do not lead you to a case in your jurisdiction, you may be able to reverse engineer a case from your jurisdiction using the procedure described in Example #1 with Shepard's Citations and the headnotes.


## ✦ Dicta Column

Legal research seems overwhelming at first, but it will get easier over time. Also take heart not worrying about the following:

✦ *That you haven't found "the great case that's out there some-where."* You make legal research more difficult when you doubt your ability and the fruits of your search. Don't make legal research harder than it is. If you find a judicial opinion or a statute that controls and is on point and you verify that it is good law, your search is over. That is what you were looking for and you found it. If you constantly worry that there must be some great case out there that you missed, you're wasting your time.

✦ *That other people have included more sources than you.* Citing fifty cases for the same proposition is a waste of time and space. As you will learn in the next chapter, brevity is a virtue in legal writing, and including a string cite of ten cases to support one legal proposition is not going to earn you points. One case that controls, is on point and good law will support any legal proposition. You just need one.

✦ *Widening your scope.* Sometimes first years think that by widening their scope (i.e. searching for cases that are outside your jurisdiction and are not on point but could be analogous if you stretched your imagination), professors will reward them for being thorough. That's not right. Your goal is to find legal authority that controls and is on point and is good law; that's all you need. Once you have that, *stare decisis* takes over and your case should be decided the way you want it to be decided. Legal research isn't like your college English class. Do not get so creative that you find yourself writing about unrelated, albeit interesting areas of the law.

+ *Using LEXIS and WESTLAW.* Some professors try to discourage first years from using electronic databases, telling them that there is no substitute for "using the books" and that if they don't learn to use the books now, they never will. The truth is, there is no easier way to determine whether a case is good law or not than by using the electronic databases. These databases also help you if for some reason a reporter is missing from the shelf and you want to read a case. Also, you can print off lists of cases that refer to your headnote from the databases, and you can find very new cases that haven't been printed in the reporters yet. You should try to become as proficient as possible in using the databases, because these skills will help you throughout law school and your legal career.

    It's true that some books such as digests, the *Index to Legal Periodicals* and the summaries of state and federal law can't be replaced by the electronic databases. Thus, your best approach is to use electronic databases and the books in tandem to complement each other.

+ *All the sources that don't relate to your issue.* Don't be overwhelmed by the volumes of sources packed into your law library or worry that you'll never learn to use them all. Law libraries contain everything from session laws to the Internal Revenue Code, foreign laws to administrative rules, U.N. documents to Common Market materials. Unless your legal research assignment focuses on one of these discrete topics, don't even worry about sources like these. Concern yourself with defining your issue ahead of time by answering the three questions you need to begin your research, then start your search for judicial opinions and statutes. Use the secondary sources listed above to help you locate judicial opinions and statutes, and don't overwhelm yourself thinking about all the sources out there that you don't know about. You don't need to know.

# CHAPTER SIX
# ✦ Legal Writing

Most law schools provide first years with some kind of instruction in legal writing. At some schools, first years get a comprehensive, thorough class that is conducted somewhat like a college composition class, where a professor or upperclassman teaches you step-by-step how to write legal documents. At other schools, you are handed a book about legal writing and are left to figure it out on your own.

Whether your school falls into one of the above categories or is somewhere in the middle, this chapter will teach you how to do the legal writing required of you in your first year of law school. The chapter is divided into three parts:

I.   First you will learn the basic structure of legal writing: issue, rule, analysis, and conclusion (or IRAC).
II.  Second, you will learn the rules for legal citation that you need to know to write your documents.
III. Third, the chapter will give you five common-sense, easy-to-learn style rules that will improve the quality of your legal writing.

The chapter ends with a sample memorandum that will give you a visual example of what legal writing looks like.


## I. IRAC: Issue, Rule, Analysis, Conclusion

IRAC is the cardinal rule of legal writing—issue, rule, analysis, conclusion. It is the conventional form for legal writing that law schools teach for both legal documents and exam answers. You will use IRAC throughout your legal career; lawyers in their memos and briefs and even judges in their opinions follow the structure of IRAC. We'll take each element in turn.

## A. Issue

The "issue" is the legal question that your document will answer. It is also sometimes referred to as the "question presented." As a rule of thumb, you want to state your issue in a single sentence, if you possibly can. An example of an issue is:

> Whether defendant is liable for fraud because she told plaintiff that Babe Ruth autographed the baseball card that plaintiff purchased.

State the issue as a sentence, rather than a question. It is usually easiest to follow the format above, beginning the sentence with "whether." The first part of the sentence ("whether defendant") identifies the party or parties, and the second part of the sentence ("is liable for fraud") identifies the law at issue. The final part of the sentence identifies the relevant facts. Limiting the issue to one sentence forces you to sort out the crucial facts from the extraneous ones.

In drafting a legal document or answering an exam question, you may be required to identify multiple issues. Law school exams, for example, often can be "issue spotting" exams, which reward the number of issues a student can spot and analyze during the time allowed to answer. When you are faced with multiple issues, take each issue in turn and state each one separately, as an individual sentence.

## B. Rule

The "rule" is the rule of law that governs the issue, and will come from either a judicial opinion or a statute. Continuing the example issue stated above, you would supply the elements of a cause of action for fraud under the rule element, because that is the rule of law that governs this particular issue. In a legal memorandum or brief, you need to cite the case or statute from which the rule came, following the *Bluebook* citation form explained in Chapter Four. On an exam answer, however, you do not need to cite a case name for the rule. An example of a rule is as follows:

> The elements of a cause of action for fraud are: (1) a misrepresentation, (2) knowledge of falsity, (3) intent to defraud (i.e., to induce reliance), (4) justifiable reliance, and (5) resulting damages. <u>Magpali v. Farmers Group, Inc.</u>, 48 Cal App. 4th 471, 484 (1996).

## C. Analysis

"Analysis" is the application of the rule to the issue to determine the outcome of the dispute. Using the facts from your question, apply the facts to the rule of law and determine whether the rule of law is satisfied. For example:

> Assuming that the plaintiff had the opportunity to see and read the card, the first four elements of a cause of action for fraud are present in this case. First, defendant falsely represented to plaintiff that the baseball card was autographed by Babe Ruth. Second, defendant knew that the representation was false because defendant admitted that he autographed it himself. Third, defendant clearly intended to induce plaintiff's reliance on the misrepresentation. He wanted to convince plaintiff to buy the card, and plaintiff told defendant that he was interested only in autographed cards. Fourth, defendant's action resulted in damage to plaintiff because plaintiff paid a thousand dollars for a card worth three dollars.
>
> However, the final element, whether plaintiff's reliance was justified, is less clear. Plaintiff is a life-long card collector who considers himself an expert in the field. Plaintiff has a Babe Ruth autographed card in his collection. A comparison of the autograph on the card and Babe Ruth's autograph shows that the two are noticeably dissimilar, and there is a question of whether plaintiff knew this or should have known that the autograph was a forgery.

The analysis section should include any assumptions or caveats that limit the analysis. For example, the above analysis assumes that the plaintiff had the ability to read the autograph. If, for example, the card were purchased over the Internet and the plaintiff could not see the autograph, the conclusion might be quite different. The analysis section also requires you to face negative facts and inferences head-on. Here, the plaintiff is an expert in the field of baseball cards, and there is a clear possibility that he should have known better than to be duped by this phony autograph. Also, your analysis section should anticipate the opposing side's counter-arguments and address them. Part of analysis is the ability to see a problem from all perspectives, evaluate the arguments and answer them as best you can.

The analysis section is your opportunity to show your professor that you understand the law, that you can see parallels and analogies between situations and that you can apply the law to a variety of different situations. Remember that on law school legal memoranda and especially on exams, there is no "right" way to analyze a problem. Your grade will reflect the quality of your analysis, not the conclusion you reach. In fact, you are entitled to come to any conclusion you want, as long as you apply the right rule and your analysis section supports your conclusion.

## D. Conclusion

The conclusion is the product of your analysis—it answers the question presented by your issue. After you have exhausted the analysis, applied the facts to the law and looked at the problem from as many perspectives as you can, write your conclusion succinctly and clearly. Don't belabor the point, and don't repeat points from your analysis section. Your reader has just finished reading your analysis and remembers what you had to say. Also, don't make your conclusion too unequivocal; remember, in a court of law, you never really know how a dispute will turn out. Just write your conclusion, say why you think the case would come out that way, and you're finished. For example:

> Assuming that plaintiff purchased the card at defendant's store and had the opportunity to inspect it, defendant is not liable for fraud because plaintiff's reliance on defendant's misrepresentation was not justifiable.

## II. The *Bluebook* Writing Rules

In addition to the citation rules you learned in Chapter Four, there are three *Bluebook* rules you need to learn for legal writing: parentheticals, introductory signals and subsequent history.

## A. Parentheticals

Parentheticals are used to give added information to the reader about the sources you cite. For example, after you provide a full cite to a case, you can write a parenthetical after the cite that explains the case and/or tells the reader why the case is relevant to your document. For example:

> Byes v. Telecheck Recovery Servs., Inc., 173 F.R.D. 421 (E.D. La. 1997) (denial of class certification in consumer credit action against collection company because plaintiff's conduct and communication with defendant was not the same as other unnamed class members).

Parentheticals usually are not required, but you can use them when you think it would help clarify things in the reader's mind. Also, when you use certain "introductory signals" (explained below), the *Bluebook* encourages you to provide information in a parenthetical.

## B. Introductory Signals

Introductory signals are abbreviations you can include before the citation of your authority (i.e. case, statute or law review article) to indicate to the reader how the authority relates to its correlating proposition in your document. When you quote directly from an authority or refer to an authority in the text of your document, do not use any introductory signal. In other instances, however, introductory signals are required. Here are the ones you need to know:

### 1. See

Use see when the cited authority "directly states" or "clearly supports" your proposition.

### 2. See also

Use see also when you cite more than one authority that directly states or clearly supports your proposition. When you use see also, the *Bluebook* encourages you to explain the particular case in a parenthetical. For example:

> Cases involving individual issues of misrepresentation and reliance are not appropriate for class treatment. See Martin v. Dahlberg, Inc., 156 F.R.D. 207, 215–17 (N.D. Cal. 1994) (stating that class actions are not appropriate for claims in which individual issues of reliance are predominate); see also In re Woodward & Lothrop Holdings, Inc., 205 B.R. 365, 371–72 (Bankr. S.D.N.Y. 1997) (gathering cases and denying class certification on claims of fraud, unjust enrichment and Pennsylvania Consumer Protection Statute).

### 3. Cf.

Use cf. to indicate that a cited authority supports a proposition different from your main proposition but nonetheless "sufficiently analogous" to also give support to your main proposition. Because you are making an analogy in using this particular authority, you should explain why the authority is analogous in a parenthetical. For example:

> "A class representative must be part of the same class and possess the same interest and suffer the same injury as the class members." Amchem Products, Inc. v. Windsor, 117 S. Ct. 2231, 2250–51, 521 U.S. 591 (1997) (citations

and internal quotations omitted); cf. Byes. v. Telecheck Recovery Servs. Inc., 173 F.R.D. 421, 424–25 (class certification denied in consumer credit action absent proof of defendant's identical conduct and communication with class representative and unnamed class members).

### 4. Compare . . . with

When you want to show that comparing two or more cases will support or illustrate your proposition, use compare . . . with. Because you want to explain to your reader why the cases are similar, you should explain them in a parenthetical.

### 5. But see

When you cite an authority that is contrary to your proposition, use but see. But see is the opposite of see.

### 6. See generally

When you cite an authority that does not specifically support your proposition but instead provides background or general information regarding the proposition, use see generally. To make clear why the authority is relevant, use a parenthetical. For example:

> Securities cases are appropriate for class treatment. See generally Schwartz v. Harp, 108 F.R.D. 279, 281 (C.D. Cal. 1985) (Rule 23 should be liberally construed in making a class determination in a securities action in recognition of the rules policy in favor of class actions).

## C. Subsequent History

Whenever you cite a case in a full citation (which you learned to do in Chapter Four), you must include all of its subsequent history. The most common things that happen are that a court affirms, reverses, modifies, vacates or withdraws a decision. Also common is whether the United States Supreme Court grants or denies certiorari.

On Table T.9 of the *Bluebook*, you will find the abbreviations for all these words. Table T.9 also shows you whether a comma is required after the various abbreviations. For example:

> Jordan v. County of Los Angeles, 669 F.2d 1311 (9th Cir.), vacated, 459 U.S. 810 (1982).

# III. The Style Rules

Citation form and IRAC are the difficult parts. What follows is the easy part, the five simple, common-sense rules that will greatly improve your legal writing.

## A. Follow the Format Rules Applicable to Your Document

This may sound silly, but the appearance of your document may have great bearing on the grade you receive on the finished product. In the real world, legal writing has strict rules of form, and if a lawyer neglects those rules, it can mean that his client loses. Circuit courts, for example, have rules of form guiding the briefs that appellants and appellees file. The United States Supreme Court demands that every document filed with it conform to a very strict format.

Therefore, when an assignment asks you to write a particular document, such as a letter to a client or a brief to a federal circuit court, make sure that you follow the form rules for that document. Many first years mistakenly believe that it matters more what they have to say than how they say it, but it doesn't work that way. In the legal world, you won't have a chance to tell people what you have to say unless you say it in the right format. So if a writing instructor assigns you a client letter to write, write a letter. It only takes a couple of minutes to follow this simple rule of form, but if your document looks right, you look like you know what you're doing. If you can't get the easy stuff right, such as simple format rules, how can you be expected to get the hard stuff right, like the content?

## B. Know Your Audience

If your instructor asks you to write a motion to dismiss pursuant to Rule 12(b)(6) of the Federal Rules of Civil Procedure, your target audience is a federal judge. If an exam question asks you to write your answer in the form of a letter to your client, make your answer look like a letter and address it "Dear Mr. So-and-So."

Also, remember that your voice will be different depending on who you're writing to. Your language will be clear, formal and serious when you address a federal court. When you write a client letter, your tone will be less formal, and you will want to include an explanation (in layman's terms, rather than sophisticated legal terms) of the various legal concepts discussed.

## C. Know Your Document

In your first year of law school, you will be asked to write two types of documents: expository documents and persuasive documents. Expository documents are intended to inform the reader. An example of an expository document is a memorandum to a member of your (hypothetical) law firm outlining your client's legal rights in response to a given set of facts. The purpose of expository documents is to educate the reader and provide an unbiased assessment of what the applicable law is and how the law applies to the given facts.

An example of a persuasive document is a brief submitted to a court. Persuasive documents are intended to convince the reader that a certain position is the correct one. You write to advocate a position and persuade the reader to adopt that position. As in expository writing, you will provide the applicable law, but in persuasive writing you will try to convince the reader that the law supports your position and that the reader should accept your conclusion. If there are cases that go against your position, however, do not ignore them. Instead, use your analytic ability to distinguish them from your set of facts.

## D. Use Headings

Legal documents are not like the compositions you wrote for your college literature classes. In legal documents, above all else you want to be clear. You want your reader to know where she is and what's going on at all times. Headings help you do this because they give your reader a road map of what each section of your document seeks to establish. Clear and concise headings underlined at the beginning of the paragraph tell your reader what she can expect to read in the upcoming section. Headings also help you write a better document, because taking the time to formulate a clear and concise heading forces you to evaluate the purpose of each section of your document and stick to that purpose.

## E. Outline Before You Begin

As you learned in Chapter Five, you must identify your issue before you begin your research. Similarly, you should outline the legal issues you plan to write about before you begin writing. Your outline also should include a thesis statement of the conclusion you want to reach (the point you want to make). Outlining the issues and developing a thesis will force you to really think about the structure of the document before you begin writing. This avoids the trap that many first years fall into, which is to wander aimlessly around in their document, talking about issues and rules but having no idea where they're going.

## ✦ Sample Memorandum

The following is a sample memorandum, written by an attorney to a member of his firm evaluating a legal question. Different law firms have different rules of form regarding memoranda, so do not take this particular form as the required form across the board.

### MEMORANDUM

Issue: Whether Company A can enforce an assignment (hereafter, the "Assignment") entered into between Employee and Company A to obtain the benefits of all improvements generated by Employee while working for Company B.

Conclusion: Yes. Although the Assignment may not be enforceable to the full extent of its terms, the Assignment effected a valid transfer of rights to Company A and Company A may seek to enforce those rights by a suit for damages or injunctive relief if Company A can establish that (1) Employee developed improvements to the particular patents he assigned to Company A, or (2) Employee developed technology for Company B using Company A's trade secrets.

I. FACTS.

Employee (hereafter, EE) was an employee and officer of Company A. Company A was in the business of manufacturing widgets. EE developed a particular technology for making widgets (hereafter, the Technology). In 1996, EE and Company A executed the Assignment. The Assignment is governed by California law and, among other things, provides:

1. CONFIRMATION OF ASSIGNMENT. EE hereby confirms, acknowledges and agrees that EE has transferred and assigned to Company A all right, title and interest of EE in and to the Technology, including the patent rights which have been developed, conceived, invented or otherwise created, acquired or owned by EE. Further, EE

presently has no rights to any intellectual property which could be considered part of or related to the Technology.

2.   FURTHER DEVELOPMENTS. EE hereby agrees and confirms that any and all improvements and other intellectual property developed, conceived, invented or otherwise created or acquired by EE, whether prior to or subsequent to the date hereof, which relates in any fashion to the Technology, patent rights or improvements, shall be the sole and absolute property of Company A, and EE shall have no right, title or interest with respect thereto.

In July 1998, Company A filed a bankruptcy petition. Beginning in October 1998, EE and company B entered into a series of Employment Agreements in which, among other things, EE stated:

I have not entered into, and I agree I will not enter into, any agreement either written or oral in conflict with this Agreement or my employment with Company B, I will not violate any agreement with or rights of any third party or, except as expressly authorized by Company B in writing hereafter, use or disclose my own or any third party's confidential information or intellectual property when acting within the scope of my employment or otherwise on behalf of Company B. Further, I have not retained anything containing any confidential information of a prior employer or other third party, whether or not created by me.

For purposes of this memorandum, I have assumed that EE's employment with Company B has included work on production of widgets and related Technology. As noted below, however, the exact nature and timing of EE's work will determine the extent of Company A's rights against EE and/or Company B.

II.   ANALYSIS.

Company A may seek a preliminary injunction against Company B based on the contractual duties owed by EE, breach of fiduciary duties owed by EE and on California statutes including the California Uniform Trade Secret Act. See IMI-Tech Corp. v. Gagliani, 691 F. Supp. 214, 229–30 (S.D. Cal. 1986). Company A's chances of obtaining a preliminary injunction will be greatest if Company A can show (1) that EE has developed improvements to a particular patented device which EE had assigned to Company B, or (2) that EE has used Company A's trade secrets to develop technology for Company B.

A.   Assignment of Rights to an Existing Patent.

EE's assignment of rights to a patent and the improvements thereto is valid and enforceable. Patents are personal property and "[a]pplications for patents, or any interest therein, shall be assignable in law by an instrument in writing." 35 U.S.C. § 261 (1988). Agreements to assign inventions and patents are specifically enforceable. Goodyear Tire & Rubber Co. v. Miller, 22 F.2d 353, 355 (9th Cir. 1927). Thus, the Assignment is valid and enforceable as it relates to existing patents and Company A has title to the patents transferred by EE to Company A.

The Assignment effectuated a valid and enforceable assignment of any technology that is an improvement upon the patents transferred by EE and was developed by EE. "An assignment of an imperfect invention, with all improvements upon it that the inventor may make, is equivalent in equity to an assignment of the perfected results." Littlefield v. Perry, 88 U.S. 205, 226–27 (1874) (discussing an assignment which, by its express terms, covered all improvements to the original patent).

> [W]here a man purchases a particular machine secured by a patent, and open to an indefinite line of improvements, it is often of great consequence to him that he should have the benefit of any future improvements that may be made to it. Without that, the whole value of the thing may be taken away from him the next day. . . . [I]t has become the practice, in many cases, to stipulate for all future improvements that may be made by the same inventor upon any particular machine which he induces a party to purchase from him, sometimes by way of license to use such improvements, and sometimes by way of purchase and ownership thereof. Where the inventor is connected in business with the party making such stipulation, or is interested in the profits arising from the business in which the invention is used, the arrangements seems to be altogether unobjectionable.

Aspinwall Mfg. Co. v. Gill, 32 F. 697, 700–01 (C.C.D.N.J. 1887) (Bradley, Circuit Justice, citing Littlefield and stating that the issue is settled law).

There are, however, two general limitations on the ability to assign the rights to future "improvements" on a patented device. First, the phrase or concept of "improvements" is likely limited to improvements to the patented device, rather than a new invention that might compete with the patented device without infringing on the patent. Universal Sales Corp. v. California Press Mfg. Co., 20 Cal. 2d 751, 767 (1942). Thus, the Assignment will not, by itself, preclude EE from developing a new and better device for making widgets.

Second, the assignment of rights in an invention which is made prior to the existence of the invention is the assignment of an expectant interest. The assignment of an expectant interest may be a valid assignment, but the assignee holds only an equitable title. Filmtec Corp. v. Allied Signal Inc., 939 F.2d 1568, 1572 (Fed. Cir. 1991). Thus, to the extent that EE has assigned the rights to future inventions other than those which had already been patented, Company A has an equitable title which is subject to being cut off by a subsequent purchaser for valuable consideration, without notice.

B.    Assignment of Rights to Future Inventions.

Company A's right to EE's future inventions (those inventions which are not "improvements" to a particular patented device) are less certain. The law disfavors abstract restrictions on an individual's rights to employment and to future intellectual property. This concern with protecting an individual's right is, however, balanced against the policy favoring protection of an employer's trade secrets and confidential information.

1.    Enforceability of "Hold-Over" Clauses.

The Assignment may be considered a species of "hold-over" clauses (also known as "trailer clauses"). A hold-over clause is "a contractual provision in which the employee-inventor agrees to assign his entire interest in any invention he creates during a period following termination of the employment relationship." Note, Unhitching the Trailer Clause: The Rights of Inventive Employees and Their Employers, 3 J. Intell. Prop. L. 187, 188 (1995). Hold-over clauses are "enforceable only if they constitute a reasonable and justifiable restriction on the right of employees to work in their profession for subsequent employers." Dorr-Oliver, Inc. v. United States, 432 F.2d 447, 452 (Ct. Cl. 1970). In particular, hold-over clauses must be limited to reasonable time periods and to subject matter which the employee worked on or had knowledge of during his employment. Id.

The Assignment in this case may violate the first condition because it contains no express time limit. As such, the assignment may be considered an unreasonable restriction on EE's ability to work in his profession for subsequent employers.

The Assignment should, however, satisfy the second condition because it is limited to patents and trade secrets of Company A in its field of business. In addition, it is reasonable to expect that EE, as an officer of Company A, should be held to a high standard of knowledge regarding all of Company A's business interests.

2.    California's Limits on Restraint of Trade.

California has two specific statutory provisions which could effect the validity of the Assignment, each of which is discussed below.

First, the Labor Code specifically limits the ability of an employer to provide for the assignment of inventions made by an employee. Section 2870 provides:

(a)   Any provision in an employment agreement which provides that an employee shall assign, or offer to assign, any of his or her rights in an invention to his or her employer shall not apply to an invention that the employee developed entirely on his or her own time without using the employer's equipment, supplies, facilities, or trade secret information except for those inventions that either:

(1)   Relate at the time of conception or reduction to practice of the invention to the employer's business, or actual or demonstrably anticipated research or development of the employer; or

(2)   Result from any work performed by the employee for the employer.

Cal. Lab. Code § 2870 (West 1998); see also Cubic Corp. v. Marty, 185 Cal. App. 3d 438, 453 (1986) (holding that § 2870 does not apply to an employee's inventions related to the employer's business).

Section 2870 of the Labor Code is probably not applicable to the Assignment in this case. The Assignment is not an "employment agreement." Instead, it is an assignment of certain technology. In addition, the focus of the Assignment is technology that was developed and used by Company A in its business. Nevertheless, there is a possibility that a court may interpret the Assignment as a form of employment agreement.

Second, California has developed a number of limitations on employment agreements. California's Business & Professions Code limits the ability of an employer to restrain the employee from competing with the employer. It provides:

Except as provided in this chapter, every contract by which anyone is restrained from engaging in a lawful profession, trade, or business of any kind is to that extent void.

Cal. Bus. & Prof. Code § 16600 (West 1998). There are no published cases that indicate whether a California court will apply either of these two statutes to our set of facts. It is reasonable, however, to expect that a California court would draw on general law relating to hold-over clauses, discussed above.

3. Protection of Trade Secrets and Confidential Information.

California's limitation on restraint of trade must be balanced against California's protection of trade secrets and confidential information. Employment agreements which seek to protect an employer's trade secrets and confidential information are generally enforceable. For example, an employment contract which requires former California employees to assign their former inventions that were conceived during their employment and within one year of termination of employment and "based upon" confidential information, is enforceable. Winston Research Corp. v. Minnesota Mining & Mfg. Co., 350 F.2d 134 (9th Cir. 1965).

On the other hand, an employment agreement which requires the former employee to assign and communicate all ideas and concepts within one year of termination of employment, regardless of whether they are based upon the employer's secrets or not, is valid and enforceable only to the extent that it relates to the ideas and concepts which were based upon secrets or confidential information of the employer and which were conceived during or within one year of employment. Armorlite Lens Co. v. Campbell, 340 F. Supp. 273 (S.D. Cal. 1972).

In addition, the California Uniform Trade Secrets Act provides that misappropriation of trade secrets is actionable in California by an action for injunction and/or damages. Cal. Civ. Code § 3426 et seq. (West 1998). Thus, it is likely that Company A will be able to enjoin EE from giving information regarding the technology to Company B if the information is considered a trade secret.

Finally, EE, as a member of management (and, in fact, an officer and majority shareholder) of Company A owed fiduciary obligations to Company A to keep secret technical information learned or created during his employment. See Winston Research, 350 F.2d at 140; IMI-Tech, 691 F. Supp. at 230.

## ✦ Dicta Column

You'll be somewhat anxious about legal writing until you get some practice or you get a good grade on one of your assignments, but for now, take heart not worrying about the following:

✦ *Using legalese.* Even though you're probably intimidated by the prospect of writing a legal document, do not fall into the trap of using legalese to make it sound like you know what you're doing. Legalese, whether it is used in a memo, brief, judicial opinion or oral argument, does not make you sound like you know what you're talking about. Instead, it's confusing, irritating and pretentious. Clarity and brevity are the hallmarks of good legal writing. It's much harder to write what you want to say in one simple, short sentence than it is to use four rambling sentences to say the same thing.

✦ *When the law goes against you.* Sometimes you get an assignment that asks you to fight a losing battle. Professors write these questions on purpose to test your ability to solve a problem when you have little or nothing to work with. Don't beat your head against a wall trying to make the problem work out the way you want it to, and do not try to make the law seem more favorable. Try to distinguish the cases as best you can, but face the facts—your client is going to lose. In your memorandum, do the best you can for him, but tell him the truth and tell the professor all the reasons why the client doesn't have a chance. Lawyers have to give their clients a realistic and balanced assessment of the law.

✦ *When you don't understand the substance of the underlying law.* Often, your writing assignments will involve complicated issues of law, such as the First Amendment, patent law or negotiable instruments. Do not, however, be unnerved—you don't need to understand all of the complexities of the underlying law to write a good memo. In fact, the less you try to broaden the assignment into related areas, the better off you'll be because you'll be less confused. Take the sample memo, for example. All the memo is concerned with is the narrow topic of assignments, not the entire body of patent law. Narrow your focus to the immediate issue that you are working with, decide what you need to understand and ignore the rest.

✦ *If you have a shaky start.* Unlike your other classes where you get one grade for the entire semester's work, in your legal research and writing class your grade will reflect your improvement over the course of the semester. So, if you write a less-than-great first paper, don't worry too much about it. As long as you take the time to learn what went wrong and talk to your instructor about how you can improve your writing, your grades will get better over the course of the semester, and your final grade will reflect that improvement.

# CHAPTER SEVEN

# ✦ Using Study Aids Effectively

Before you even have a chance to look over the study aids available to you in your law school bookstore, your professors probably will warn you against using them. "Study aids will not help you study for my class," they'll tell you. But that's not true. The truth is that study aids can and will help you, as long as you use them correctly.

If study aids can help you tackle the rigors of law school, why do your professors discourage their use so adamantly? The simple answer is that your professors want you to toil under the Socratic Method and figure out everything on your own. Your Civil Procedure professor wants you to pore over the Federal Rules of Civil Procedure and puzzle out how those rules work and which rules apply at what stage in a trial. Your Criminal Law professor wants you to struggle with the difference between embezzlement and larceny. Your Contracts professor wants you to ponder the nuances of the concept of consideration. That's the only way to learn, they'll tell you. No pain, no gain.

To some extent, that's true, but not to the degree your professors tell you. You need to do the work yourself; you need to read your casebooks, brief your cases, go to class, make outlines and study for your exams. However, when you really don't understand something, yet have spent hours trying to figure it out, you hit the point of diminishing returns. Instead of working productively, you bang your head against a wall, spinning your wheels. There is such a thing as trying too hard to learn through the Socratic Method the things you don't understand.

This is when study aids come to your rescue, because study aids can give you simple answers to the questions that the Socratic Method asks. In one sentence, a study aid can tell you the difference between larceny and embezzlement, and you'll never confuse the two again. Study aids can help you put to memory an incredible amount of information and show you how a series of rules work together as a doctrine.

Study aids are not a replacement for reading and briefing cases, but as a supplement to your work, they can help you enormously, as long as you:

I.   Use them correctly
II.  Know what study aids are available

This chapter will explain.

# I. The Correct Way to Use Study Aids

Before you consult a study aid or even learn about what study aids are available to you, you need to learn the basic guidelines governing the use of study aids. In order to use study aids correctly, you must remember two things:

✦ *Study aids are not a replacement for your casebook reading, briefing and outlining.* Study aids augment your work; they do not replace it. Study aids can't teach you to read cases critically, synthesize information and analyze variations and extensions of the law. You learn those skills only by reading and briefing cases. You should consult study aids after you have completed your assignments, not before.

✦ *Don't overdo it.* With study aids, the rule is that less is more. Your professors assign you more than enough work to begin with, and every time you consult a study aid, you add to your workload. So remember: Don't overdo it. Instead, be very selective in choosing which study aids to let into your life.

Most law students do not know these guidelines, and consequently using study aids hurts rather than helps them. Lazy students violate rule number one. They shirk their workload and use study aids as a replacement for doing the work themselves. These students mistakenly believe that reading a canned brief is as good as briefing cases on their own. They think that reading a commercial outline is a satisfactory alternative to making their own outlines.

Overachievers, on the other hand, violate rule number two. In addition to doing the work they are assigned, these students increase their workload exponentially by consulting a whole slew of study aids. By tripling or even quadrupling their workload, overachievers exhaust themselves by making an already onerous workload overwhelming.

Don't let study aids hurt you. Remember the two guidelines: you need to do the work you're assigned, and you need to be selective in deciding which study aids to use. Now that you know the guidelines, you're ready to learn more about study aids.

## II. What Study Aids Are Available

When you bought your books at the law school bookstore, you probably noticed an entire section, almost as big as the textbook section, devoted entirely to "study aids." You saw commercial outlines, flash cards, flow-charts, Hornbooks, Nutshells and audio tapes. Some study aids are as large and dense as your casebooks themselves; others are one-page laminated charts. Still others are little paperback books that fit in your pocket. There are so many study aids to choose from that it's difficult for first years to know where to start. Which study aids are the best? Do you buy one or two or all of them? Should a study aid track the contents of your casebook? Read on. By the time you finish this chapter, you will know what the different study aids have to offer, how to use them and when to use them.

Before you go to the bookstore to look at the available study aids, take a few moments to think about your classes. What is you favorite class? By favorite, we don't mean the one you like best, we mean the one you find easiest to understand. Think about that class. How has the semester been for you? Do you feel somewhat comfortable with the material? Do you understand what's going on (even to a minimal degree)? Maybe you even understand some class discussion? If the answers to those questions are generally positive, it's very likely that you don't need a study aid for that class. You have a decent grasp on the material and are doing fine with the casebook reading alone. When this happens, don't add to your workload by taking on a study aid for that class. If this is true for more than one class, great. Continue with your reading, briefing and going to class, and consider yourself lucky that you understand one or maybe even a couple of your classes.

But what about the other ones? The classes that leave you baffled after class discussion? The ones that just don't make sense to you? The ones you spend hours wrestling with but still don't get? These are the classes that are prime candidates for the help of a study aid. It may be one class, it may be all four. One word of caution, however: In making the decision which classes you will augment with study aids, remember the rule that less is more.

Once you have decided which classes you are going to supplement with study aids, go to the study aid section of your bookstore. As you peruse the study aids, think about what you want in a study aid. Do you want something you can consult once you've briefed a case to make sure you got all the salient points? Or do you want something that will help you see the big picture of how an entire doctrine of law works together? Do you want something that will explain to you in plain English what's going on in a particular class? Perhaps you want all these things?

As you flip through the different study aids, decide which ones appeal to you. Do you like the page layout? The typeface? Do you like the weight and quality of the paper? What about the format? Does the study aid seem organized and easy to read? All these things are important in choosing a study aid. If it doesn't look appealing and understandable to you at first glance, it never will. It's important that you like the format of the study aid you choose, because you're going to spend quite a bit of time with it. And, choosing a study aid is one of those rare moments in law school when a decision is entirely up to you, so take advantage of it and pick the one you like the best.

To help you make up your mind, the following section contains descriptions that tell you more of what each study aid has to offer.

## A. Commercial Outlines

Commercial outlines are by far the most popular type of study aid. Almost all law students consult a commercial outline at some point in their law school careers. All commercial outlines perform basically the same task: They summarize a subject of law and put the whole class into an outline form. There are many to choose from: Emanuel Law Outlines, Gilbert Law Summaries, Legalines, Casenote Legal Briefs, Emanuel's Professor Series, Blond's Law Guides, Black Letter Series, Sum & Substance, Casebook Outlines, Student Guide Series, Study Partner, Aspen Law & Business and Roadmap Law Course Outlines, to name a few. Some, such as Emanuel, Gilbert and Legalines, are very long; they track the contents of your casebook, provide briefs of the cases and organize the material into a lengthy, comprehensive outline. They are not substitutes for doing your own outlines, however, because they are much too long to be useful to you. Further, they cover your entire casebook, whereas you probably will not cover even two-thirds of the casebook in your class.

The best thing about commercial outlines is that they give you quick, easy answers. If you come across a case that you just don't understand and have no idea how to brief, a commercial outline will provide you with the issue and holding. If you have trouble figuring out the significance a case has in the grand scheme of things, your commercial outline will tell you. Commercial outlines also help you relate cases to one another and show you how cases work together to form a body of law.

## B. Nutshells

Nutshells are little paperback books that give you a bare-bones account of an area of the law. They do not follow a particular casebook edition, nor are they organized in outline form. Nutshells are written in block prose and read like a book. They do not contain case briefs. In fact, Nutshells rarely go into cases in depth; they give you the holdings of a handful of cases, but if a Nutshell spends time discussing a case, it's because the case is a seminal one that is an essential component of that particular subject. Nutshells just tell you the law, in plain English, which means that you can learn a great deal from a Nutshell in a short period of time. If you find that you truly do not understand a class and are spending what you think is way too much time battling with it, take a few hours and read a Nutshell. The streamlined account of what's really going on should clear up your confusion.

## C. Hornbooks

As short as Nutshells are, Hornbooks are long. They are treatises—lengthy, considered looks at a single subject of law. The purpose of Hornbooks is to explain a subject thoroughly, from its historical roots to the current state of the law. Hornbooks are the law school version of the textbooks you used in college. They summarize the important aspects of cases, tell you what each case means, explain how the case fits into that particular area of the law and give legal commentary on whether or not the case is considered a good decision.

Sounds pretty good, right? It's true that Hornbooks are a great resource. Their only drawback is that they're long—too long, in fact, for you to read on a regular basis. It's probably not possible and certainly not smart for you to do all your casebook reading and read the applicable parts of the Hornbook as well. You would literally double your workload, and you know better than to do that. Further, there is the added danger that because Hornbooks are more interesting reading than your casebooks, you might find yourself reading the Hornbook instead of your casebook.

You need to use Hornbooks wisely, which means using them sparingly. When you have read all of your assigned reading but still don't understand what's going on, take a few minutes to read the applicable section of the Hornbook. Read only as much of the Hornbook as you need to address a specific question or topic, maybe five or ten pages. That's it. Law school libraries carry the entire Hornbook series, and you may want to forego buying Hornbooks and use the library's instead, because Hornbooks are as expensive as casebooks.

## D. Audio Tapes

Although there are audio tapes available for almost every class, the truth is that they are really only helpful for what are called "rules classes." Rules classes require you to learn a set of rules. Your first year, you will take two rules classes, Civil Procedure and Criminal Law. Audio tapes do not lend themselves to theory classes, like Torts, Contracts or Constitutional Law, because tapes can't teach you theory or how to think. Instead, tapes help you memorize, and that is what you need for rules classes.

Tapes have a format different from any other study aid. If you choose to use tapes, you'll have to give yourself over to the tapes' process and memorize the way they teach you to memorize. Tapes do not track the progression of your casebook and rarely discuss cases at all. Instead, tapes teach you the rules and the rules only. Most use "mnemonics," a memory device that assigns words to help trigger your memory of certain information, and this can be a very effective way to memorize a great deal of information. Although most audio tapes are long (six to nine hours generally) the advantage of tapes is that you can get out of the library to use them. Put a tape in your portable cassette player and walk around the neighborhood or go to the gym. If you really concentrate on the information the tapes are feeding you, you will learn a substantial amount of information and get a breath of fresh air at the same time. Once you have listened to the tapes all the way through, you may want to make a short outline of the information contained in the tapes to further help your memorizing process. Listen to the tapes as many times as you think you need to memorize the information they contain. That may be twice, it may be ten times, but no matter how often you listen to tapes, the more you concentrate, the faster you'll learn.

## E. Flash cards

If you need to put a lot of information to memory for a rules class or a closed-book exam, flash cards can be an effective way to do it. Emanuel's "Law in a Flash" series offers flash cards for almost every law school subject. Also available is the "Study Partner 720" series.

Although the flash cards made by study aid retailers are perfectly fine, you will learn the information you need to know more quickly if you make your own flash cards. Why? Because reading the information, synthesizing its content, putting the information into your own words and writing it on a card embeds the information in your memory. The process of making your own flash cards does as much to help you learn the information as going through the cards over and over again.

## F. Flowcharts

There are several different kinds of flowcharts to choose from, such as Barcharts, Foldeez Law Outlines and Little Brown & Company's "Mates." They are all basically the same—colorful, one-page laminated charts that contain the critical components of a particular class.

Flowcharts are helpful when you find yourself overloaded with rules and theories but cannot see how they fit together, a problem sometimes called "not seeing the forest for the trees." Flowcharts show you how the individual rules fit together and work as a whole. A good example of a flowchart-friendly class is Civil Procedure. A flowchart can show you which rules apply when an action is filed, when it goes to court and after judgment is entered. By identifying what rules apply at the various stages of a lawsuit, a flowchart helps you see how the rules work in the big picture. Another advantage of flowcharts is that because space is limited, they contain only essential information. This means that flowcharts show you what are the most important elements of a certain class and what are the elements to consider as you approach an exam question. Finally, because they are so concise, flowcharts demand almost no time to work with. Most of them have three holes punched in them so you can stick them in the back of your binder and refer to them whenever the mood strikes you. Flowcharts fit into your study aid plan of "less is more"; they pack a lot of information into a small area and take very little time to deal with.

## G. Bar Review Outlines

After you graduate, you will probably take a test-preparation course like "Bar-Bri" or "Bar Passers" to help you prepare for a state Bar exam. To help you study, these courses provide you with outlines of every law school course that appears on the Bar exam.

Students studying for the Bar are not the only people who can purchase these outlines, however. Anyone can buy them for a rather steep price, and some first-year law students do that. It's not, however, the best idea. While these outlines are comprehensive and well organized, they are not geared to meeting the needs of a first-year law student. Because their aim is to refresh a graduated law student's memory rather than to teach a class from the beginning, Bar review outlines are both too concise and too sophisticated to help you with your first-year classes. They contain only the bare bones of a class and assume that you already have a large base of general knowledge from which to draw. As a first year, your aim is to learn the class in the first place. Bar review outlines, however, will not help you do that. If you want to consult a commercial outline, use one of the many available to you in your law school bookstore.

## H. Student Outlines

Sympathetic upperclassmen often give their old outlines to first years, and at some point in the semester, someone probably will offer you an old outline. Using someone else's outline instead of making your own outline will do you more harm than good, but using a worthwhile one to augment your own outlining process can be helpful.

To determine whether the outline is worthwhile and likely to help you, consider the following questions. If the answers to the questions are pretty positive and on the whole you think the outline looks good, you should use it to supplement your outlining process. Use it as little or as much as you think is helpful. Any outline that gives you even one or two helpful pieces of information is worth your time.

✦ *Did the student have your professor?* If the student who prepared the outline did not have the same professor you have for a class, do not use the outline. Different professors assign different reading and stress different aspects of every class. Only if the student had your professor can you be certain that the outline covers the material you need to learn. In addition, even if the answer to this question is yes, you should still go through the outline to see whether the professor covered the same material.

✦ *When did the student take the class?* The law is always changing, and if the outline is more than two years old, it's likely that you will have to spend a lot of time bringing it up to date. Ideally, you are looking for an outline from the previous year, to keep your updating time to a minimum.

✦ *Is the outline organized in a way you understand?* Usually you can understand your own mess, but understanding someone else's mess is nearly impossible. If the outline looks a mess and you have trouble understanding its organization, don't use it—it's not a good use of your time.

Another thing to watch out for is shorthand. Many law students develop their own shorthand for certain recurring words and concepts, and if you don't understand their shorthand, you might find yourself wasting a lot of time just trying to decipher the outline.

+ *What grade did the student get in the class?* This is by no means a critical element because, as you will learn in Chapter Ten, students who study hard and do everything right, including making great outlines, can get less than stellar grades in their classes due to a lack of exam-writing skills. But just to be on the safe side, it's probably a good idea to avoid a student's outline if he received lower than a B in the class. Why study from something that didn't do even the student who made it that much good?

## I. Legal Dictionaries

Every first year should buy a legal dictionary, because during law school, you will run across hundreds of words and terms that you've never seen before. One of these days your professor will call on you thinking you didn't take the time to find out what *sine qua non* means, and if you use a legal dictionary with any regularity, you'll know the answer. You should also refer to the Glossary at the back of this book for the words and terms you will see over and over in law school and really should learn rather than look up over and over again. By the way, *sine qua non* is one of them.

Your law school bookstore carries several different legal dictionaries. Traditionally, everyone used *Black's Law Dictionary*, a large hardcover dictionary that defines almost every word you will come across in law school. Now there is a smaller paperback edition of *Black's* that is easier to carry around. Whichever dictionary you choose, use it often.

## J. Practice Exam Guides

Newer on the study aid scene are the study aids that give you exam questions to practice on before you take your finals. Siegel's, Blond's, Study Partner, Issue Spotting and Finals Law School Exam Series all contain exam questions to test your knowledge and model answers against which you can evaluate your performance.

While these books look like a good idea, they're not, for three reasons. First and foremost, law school exams do not lend themselves to standardization. Every law professor has his own take on a particular class and writes his own kind of exam question. Take your Torts professor, for example. He may have a real fascination with the concept of proximate cause, and you may have spent weeks of classes studying the contours of proximate cause. Consequently, chances are at least one of his exam questions will focus on proximate cause. But chances are also that your commercial exam question will not. Instead, the commercial exam question will be a standard, issue-spotting Torts exam. It's not practice for you to take that commercial exam. Instead, it's a waste of time, because your exam will be nothing like that.

Second, law school exams are timed exams. As you will see in Chapter Ten, the exam answers you write will not be pretty little essays like the ones you wrote in high school and college. On your law school exams, you will write as well as you can given your tough time constraints. By contrast, model answers in the commercial exam books are not real exam answers. They are pretty little essays that the authors took their time writing. If you adhere to the time constraints suggested by the commercial exam question, the model answer is going to be better than the answer you write, no matter what. Comparing your answer to the model answer is not a fair comparison. You should not demoralize yourself right before your exam week by comparing your exam-writing skills to an author who not only took his time writing the answer, but also made up the question.

Third, every law school professor edits out different aspects of a course. Take Torts again, for example. Tort law is so vast that there is no way your professor could teach you every facet of tort law in one semester. Almost all professors will teach basics like negligence, but after that, it's up for grabs. Some professors teach medical malpractice, some don't. Some teach the intentional torts, some don't. You get the picture. Chances are that in any commercial exam question, you're going to see some issues that pertain to areas of the law that you didn't cover in your class. It will only frustrate you to try to answer these exam questions. Thinking about areas of the law that you never learned diverts your focus and does nothing but confuse you. Time-wasting, focus-blurring, demoralizing and frightening is not what you are looking for in a study aid. Exams are difficult enough. Don't make things harder for yourself by consulting a commercial exam book.

Instead, take advantage of the old exams and sample answers that most professors put on file in your library. These are the best practice you can do for any exam. Every professor is different and writes different kinds of exams, and you will benefit enormously by familiarizing yourself with his particular style before you take the real exam. Further, professors tend to ask the same type of questions year after year and want the same type of response. They've even been known to repeat questions once in a while.

They very best thing you can do to prepare for exams is to take a practice exam several weeks before the exam and then go over it with your professor during office hours. Hardly any first years think to do this, but if they did, their grades would be much better. Office hours is the one time that you can get your professor's undivided attention and advice on how he wants his exam answered, and this insight is invaluable. Ask him what you did right and wrong. Ask how you could improve your answer. Ask how he grades the exam, what he gives points for and how the curve will work. Knowing the answers to these questions will tell you not only how to answer his exam, but how to study for it.

If your professor chooses not to put exams on file, however, don't panic. None of your classmates will have prior exams to practice on. You still have a leg up on the competition, however, because you know better than to buy a book of commercial exam questions.

## ✦ Dicta Column

As with every aspect of law school, there are things you shouldn't worry about when it comes to study aids, such as:

✦  *The person in your class who uses three different study aids in addition to doing all the casebook reading.* You already know what we are going to tell you: Do not think twice about this person. In every class there are the workhorses who do nothing but study, all day every day. As you learned in Chapter Two's lesson on case briefing and will learn in the next chapter on outlining, the amount of time a person spends studying is not an accurate reflection of how much that person is learning. The point of study aids is to reduce your workload. If somebody wants to quadruple the already onerous workload of the first year of law school, let him. You know better.

✦  *That you still don't understand something, even after reading the study aid.* Everyone has times in law school when they just don't understand something. No matter how many times you read a passage or how many people try to explain a concept to you, you still don't get it. In Civil Procedure it may be joinder. In Contracts it may be consideration. It can be anything. If this happens, don't panic.

Instead, take advantage of your professor's office hours. Go in and ask him the questions you have. Ask him to explain to you, in plain English, the concepts you don't understand. More than likely, he will take pity on you and will give you the real deal. Keep asking questions until you understand. Although in class professors often go out of their way to hide the ball, during office hours is the one time when professors tend to relent and spoon-feed you what you need to know. Take advantage of it.

✦  *That the commercial outline's briefs sound better than yours.* The wording a commercial outline uses may sound better or more professional than yours, but never copy case briefs from a commercial outline. You need to compose your own case briefs. Your words are yours, and you will remember your words better than those in the commercial outline.

✦ *Students who read study aids cover to cover.* One of the basic rules of using study aids is that you should read only the sections that relate to what you are covering in class. This should go without saying, but sometimes you will run across a student who boasts of reading study aids cover to cover, including sections covering topics that your professor chose not cover in class. Not only is this a waste of time, it's stupid. You have more than enough to study in your first year of law school without looking for extra work. Studying extraneous information will not help you get a better grade on your exam, because professors don't want to read about things they chose not to teach you. Moreover, studying things you don't have to learn will deduct from the time you have to study what you do need to learn. So if someone brags to you about reading extraneous information, ignore it.

✦ *That you'd learn more using study aids than you will by doing the work yourself.* Even if you get yelled at in class for not knowing answers or you don't understand things that other students seem to have no trouble with, don't decide that you can't do the work yourself and resolve to use study aids exclusively instead. Even if you're having trouble with your workload, you are still learning just by doing it yourself. You won't learn by using study aids alone in your first year of law school. You need to battle through your reading and briefing, and only after you have done the work should you consult your study aids. That's the cardinal rule of using study aids correctly, and don't let self-doubt drive you to break that rule.

## CHAPTER EIGHT
# ✦ Outlining

Like reading and briefing cases, outlining is crucial to getting good grades in law school. There's no way around it; you must make outlines for every one of your classes. Using a commercial outline or some upperclassman's old outline won't work. You have to make your own.

Your professors are not, however, going to teach you how to outline. Outlining is yet another feat that your professors expect you to teach yourself how to perform. No one will tell you at what point in the semester to begin outlining. No one will tell you what your outlines should include. Many of you have never seen an outline, and your professors are not going to show you what one is supposed to look like.

Because no one teaches you how to outline and because so much is riding on your ability to do it, most first years panic at the mere thought of outlining. Some manifest their panic by starting to outline the first week of school, working on them constantly during the semester and ending up with two-hundred-plus page outlines. Others manifest their outlining fear by procrastinating. A week or two before the exam these people finally get it together, jot down a few notes on a legal pad and call it an "outline." Neither one of these approaches, of course, is a good one. Outlining is like many of the other tasks required of you in law school—difficult, important and required. You have no choice but to outline. This chapter will teach you how. Here you will learn:

I.   What outlines are
II.  The difference between open- and closed-book exams
III. What your goals are in outlining
IV.  How and when to get started
V.   How to organize and format your outlines

At the end of the chapter is a sample Criminal Law outline to show you what all these outlining lessons look like in practice.

## I. Outlines: What Are They?

Your outlines are the product of all the reading, briefing and studying you've done over the course of the semester. They are how you study for your final exams. You won't study for your exams from your notes, casebook, briefs or study aids. You will study from your outlines. By the time you walk into your exam room, you should know your outlines inside and out.

Because your outlines are the only things you will study from for your exams, your outlines must contain all of the essential elements of every class. Every important case, every rule of law, every legal theory and doctrine, every argument and idea that you learned during the semester will appear in your outlines. But that does not mean you'll create a rambling, 200-page morass of information. Instead, you will condense, boil down, organize and simplify all that information into a cohesive, organized and easy-to-follow outline.

## II. Open- and Closed-book Exams

Although most students think that closed-book exams are more difficult than open-book, they're not exactly right. The truth is that in law school, the difference between open- and closed-book exams is not that great. While closed-book exams require you to memorize information and open-book exams allow you the comfort of your outline, the playing field is leveled to a great extent by the way the two exams are graded. The professor grading a closed-book exam isn't going to require or expect every one of your answers to be absolutely perfect. Of course your professor expects you to know the material, but she also will cut you some slack if your memory isn't absolutely 100% perfect. On the other hand, the professor grading an open-book exam does require perfection. If you have the luxury of having the answer right front of you in your outline, you'd better get the answer exactly right.

The studying process for open- and closed-book exams is also very similar. For the most part, you will have memorized your outline by the time you take the exam regardless of whether that exam is open- or closed-book, for two reasons. First, even for an open-book exam, you will have studied your outline so intently by the time the exam comes that you will have memorized more of it than you realize. Second, the reality is that on open-book exams, you need to memorize some information, because you won't have time to look up all the answers. You have too much writing to do to spend time looking though your outline, trying to find answers that you can't remember. If you have to search through your outline looking for the answer to each question, you won't have time to finish your exam.

## III. The Goals of Outlining

As you gear up to start outlining, remember the primary goals of outlining: to organize and condense. For each of your classes, you have read hundreds of pages of material. You have gone to class all day every day for weeks. You have stacks of case briefs and class notes in your binder and you may have consulted a study aid. You've spent the semester compiling an enormous amount of information—so enormous, in fact, that it's unruly and unhelpful. You need to sort through that information, organize and condense it into a manageable, workable, organized format—an outline. Organize and condense. For every outline, whether your exam is open- or closed-book, your job is to organize and condense.

How do you organize and condense? The only way is to think. Think. More than any other task in law school, outlining requires you to think. In order to condense volumes of rules, theories, doctrines and codes, you have to think. To organize those items into a workable framework that you can understand, memorize and use to answer the questions on your final exams, you need to think.

This is where most law students make a massive error. They outline without thinking. Why? Because most law students will do anything in the world to avoid thinking. Rather than sitting down and just thinking about the material, they'll consult five study aids, read cases three times each, look up obscure references to archaic legal terms in the library and (worst of all) recopy their class notes for hours on end. Then they write everything down in any order that strikes them. They're very busy, yes. But what are they accomplishing? Only one thing—avoiding having to think. Refusing to think hurts them. You've seen these people around. They study all the time, never take a break to go to dinner or the movies, just work and work, all day, all night. It's a little unnerving, because when you see people working like dogs, it's a natural reaction to think that they must be learning more than you.

They're not learning more than you. Remember the three magic words of successful outlining: organize, condense and think. Your outlining goal is to organize and condense, and the only way you can do that is by thinking.

## IV. How and When to Get Started

Some students start outlining the first day of the semester and some begin two days before the exam. The latter is obviously too late, and the first, maybe not so obviously, is much too early. Before you start outlining, you need to have learned enough so that you can see a connection between some of the things you've learned and see how they work together so you can organize. This means that before you jump into outlining, you need to go through several weeks of the semester and cover some material. If you have two sets of exams, in December and May, the general rule is to start outlining after one-half of the semester has gone by. This both gives you something to go on when you start outlining and leaves you plenty of time to complete all your outlines before exam week. If you only have exams at the end of the year, you should start outlining within the first three or four weeks of the spring semester.

Once you start outlining, you have to keep up with it. This means that in addition to the reading and briefing you do every day, you will also have to outline. Once you start your outlines, keeping up with them and continuing to add to them becomes additional homework that you must do consistently throughout the semester. It's easier for you to outline certain concepts when they are fresh in your mind, and if you wait and try to do all your outlines at once at the end of the semester, you'll never finish them all.

Another related question students ask is when they should finish outlining. Ideally, you want your outlines to be finished at the beginning of your study week or "reading week," so that you have plenty of time to study and memorize them. But because professors have a tendency to dump a lot of material on students during the final classes of the semester, outlining during reading week is sometimes unavoidable. If this happens, don't panic. Don't ignore that material, either. If your professor took the time to squeeze that particular material into the last days of the semester, it is likely that the material will be on the exam. All this will factor into when you finish your outlines, but ideally you should try finish your outlines as soon as you can so that you have at least a few days of reading week to study your completed outlines.

Once the semester hits the halfway point and you think you're ready to start, pick a day to start outlining. Weekends are probably best, because you can start fresh in the morning and work uninterrupted until you're done. Choose a Saturday or a Sunday and pick a class to start outlining. You might want to start with your favorite class, because you understand it best and will be able to concentrate on teaching yourself to outline.

When the designated day comes, wake up early. If you drink coffee, make a big pot. Turn down the ringer on your telephone. Sit at your desk and arrange around you all of your class paraphernalia: casebook, case briefs, class notes, study aids and any outlines you got from upperclassmen. Take out a clean sheet of paper or turn on your computer and open a new document. Work in your normal handwriting or twelve-point typeface. Don't write small and pack as much on the page as you can, because you need to be able to read this document. Work in single space, using double spaces to separate paragraphs. At the top of the page, write the name of the class in block capitals and underline it. Your outline is begun.

That's all you'll write for quite a while, however. Before you start writing your outline, you need to figure out how you're going to organize it. Remember the rules: organize, condense, think. Because everyone is different, everyone organizes outlines in a different way. There is no right or wrong way to organize an outline. You can arrange the material in countless different ways, any of which might work for you. Your job is to figure out which way that is.

# V. Organization

There are two components of organization: how you organize the material you covered in class, and how you format your outline. Before you start worrying about formatting, you need to decide how you will tackle the organization.

## A. Organizing the Material

The first question you will face as you sit down to outline is where to begin. With weeks and weeks worth of notes, where do you start? The answer is, of course, to think about it. Before you write anything, take some time to think about your class. Where does the class logically begin in your mind? Maybe it began where the professor started on the first day of class. Maybe the casebook's table of contents shows you where beginning is. Maybe your study aid can tell you where the beginning is.

If you have trouble deciding where to start, take out a sheet of scratch paper and list the different things you have learned in class. Try to fit together the different things you've learned. For example, in Civil Procedure you may have studied Rule 12(b)(6) motions, jurisdiction, complaints and answers. How do these elements fit together? Well, before an answer you have to have a complaint. Before you bring a 12(b)(6) motion there must be a complaint, because a 12(b)(6) motion is a motion to dismiss. Before you file a complaint, there has to be jurisdiction. So, jurisdiction comes first, then the complaint and 12(b)(6) motion. Last would be the answer. Where does your outline begin? With jurisdiction.

Like Civil Procedure, Contracts has a kind of framework to it. Say you've studied remedies for breach of contract, offer, breach and acceptance. Where would you begin? With offer, right? Because before you even consider remedies, you need to have offer, acceptance and a breach.

Why is it so important to see the framework of a class? Because the framework is how you will answer the questions on your exam. Think about it. Your exam questions will be hypothetical situations that present different issues of law for you to discuss in your answer. How do you approach any problem? At the beginning. For example, say your exam goes something like this: A man tells a woman he'll paint her house for fifty dollars. She pays him the money but he only paints half the house, and what he does paint he paints badly. Now she wants her fifty dollars back. Discuss.

This is a remedies question, right? Sure it is. But before you jump in and discuss remedies, you need to start at the beginning. Do these people have a contract? To answer that, you need to go back and see whether there is an offer. Then you determine whether there was an acceptance. Next you determine whether there was a breach. Only if the answer to all these questions is yes do you get to the issue of remedies.

You have to start at the beginning. Because you approach every legal question at the beginning, whether it's an exam hypothetical or a new case you've received as a lawyer, you should learn subjects from the beginning. Structuring your outlines this way trains you to approach every problem at the beginning. In your exam room, just looking at the way your outline is structured will remind you not to jump in and start answering the question in the middle, but to analyze the problem from start to finish.

Try not to worry too much if as you start outlining you have a lot of trouble seeing the framework of classes. Remember that you will get better at it over time, and it will never be as difficult to organize material as it is the first semester. Also, take heart in the fact that there are some classes where it's easy to decide where to start, simply because it doesn't really matter. Criminal Law is one of those classes. Say that so far this semester you have studied robbery, larceny, embezzlement, murder, manslaughter and negligent homicide. As you draw them on your scratch paper, you'll probably see that these crimes fit together in two distinct areas: theft crimes and homicide. But none of the crimes really comes before the other, in a "framework" sense. The facts of the exam question will tell you where to begin approaching the problem. If someone dies, you know to start with homicide. If someone gets her purse taken, you start with theft. So, one of your headings is "Theft Crimes," with the subheadings of robbery, larceny and embezzlement. Under the "Homicide" heading comes murder, manslaughter and negligent homicide. It doesn't matter whether homicide or theft comes first in your outline.

## B. Formatting Your Outline

Regardless of whether your exam is open- or closed-book, the most important formatting rule is to make your outline user-friendly. All your outlines must be easy to study from and easy to understand. In addition, outlines for open-book exams also need to be especially easy to maneuver, because you need to be able to find what you're looking for quickly and easily. You need a table of contents. You need to make sure different sections are clearly labeled. You need to write essential rules of law in good, workable sentences that you can copy straight out of your outline and into your blue book. Also, you should tab the outline so you can turn to the page you want in a matter of seconds. All these things save time, and you will appreciate this as you madly write in your blue books.

For both open- and closed-book exams, these are the ten format rules you should follow as you make your outlines.

### 1. Make Your Outlines Pretty

This sounds trivial, but it's actually one of the most important aspects of outlining. If an outline is easy on the eye, it's easier to read, memorize and use an exam. Our brains are accustomed to reading standardized text. When we pick up a book, magazine or newspaper, we easily process the information it contains, because the text is standardized and our eyes know what to expect before we even start reading. We like to look at single-spaced text with paragraphs separated by double spaces. We like short paragraphs and bite-size chunks of information, because they're easier to understand and remember. We find it difficult to remember chunks of information if they are split up from one page to the next, so keep your paragraphs together, even if it means leaving some white space at the end of the page. Make things easy on yourself by making your outlines easy on the eye.

### 2. Use Your Typeface Options

Underline, italics, bullets, capitals and boldface are enormously useful in creating consistent, easy-to-understand outlines that are easy on the eye. Rather than having one morass of generic single-spaced Roman text, these keys allow you to distinguish and set off different parts of your outline. Section headings can be in boldface type, so you always know where you are. Rules of law can be capitalized or underlined. Italics can set off important arguments. Items in a series can be set off with bullets. Be creative with your typewriter keys and make your outlines easy to understand and memorize.

### 3. Make Your Outlines Consistent

Consistency makes your outlines easier to read, understand and memorize. If you decide to write your rules of law in capital letters to distinguish them from the text around them, then remember always to write your rules of law in capital letters. If you use boldface type to indicate a new topic, always remember when to use your boldface type. However you decide to write your outline, being consistent means that you will be able to rely on your outlines and know what you're reading.

### 4. Use Standard Outlining Conventions

The standard outlining conventions are: I., A., 1., a., i). Learn them now, and it will save you time in the long run. If you consistently use the standard outlining conventions, you will always know where you are in your outline, no matter what page you open it up to. These conventions organize your outline in a consistent way, and you'll never find yourself wondering where you are or what comes next in your outline.

### 5. Leave Lots of White Space

In your effort to make your outlines as succinct as possible, do not try to cram as much information as you can on the page. An outline is not a crib sheet; it is the guide to an entire semester's work. In order to be easy on the eye, the pages of your outline need to have lots of white space. Double space between paragraphs. If a paragraph gets long, split it in two. Triple space between different sections.

### 6. Number the Elements of Rules of Law

When a rule of law has different elements, break them down—literally. Give each element a number. Not only will this help you memorize the rule, on the exam it will show you in black and white the elements you need to consider in your answer. Look at the sample outline at the end of this chapter to see how this works.

### 7. Be Careful of Shorthand

Everybody uses shorthand in their outlines, because it doesn't make sense to write out "plaintiff" or "defendant" or "contract" fifty million times. "P" and "D" and "K" work just as well. Do not, however, develop so many shorthand devices that the outline becomes unintelligible. You need to be able to understand your outline, even in the middle of what is sure to be a stressful exam.

### 8. Write in Complete Sentences

Not every sentence of your outline needs to be a complete one, but use complete sentences whenever you can, especially when stating rules of law. It may take more time to write your outline this way, but for two reasons you'll be happy that you did. First, you will practically memorize your outline by the time you finish studying for your exam. If you memorize complete sentences, you will have those sentences on the tip of your tongue during your exam. You won't waste a second of your time thinking "How should I write this?" because you'll have the sentence in your head and ready to go on the page. Second, if your memory doesn't serve you well on your exam, you can turn to your outline and copy straight out of it. You will save time and brainpower on your exam if you take the time while you are outlining to use complete sentences.

### 9. Make Only One Outline

Some first years make more than one outline for each class—a long outline, a medium-sized outline and a really short outline. The theory is that the long outline contains more than you need to know, the medium one contains what you need to know, and the short one is just a little reminder outline.

This is not an effective use of your time. Instead, it's another device students use to avoid having to think. You need only one outline, one that contains what you need to know and nothing else. The repeat costs of making two or three outlines aren't worth it. Spend your time making one outline that contains everything you need to know, condensed and organized. That's it.

### 10. Extract

Include only what's important. No facts, no little tidbits from cases, no legal history, no out-of-date rules, no archaic legal terms. Don't include case names unless the case is a seminal one (in which case you should already know it) or if it triggers your memory of the rule of law. And never include material that you did not cover in class. You will not be tested on things your professor didn't cover. Moreover, most professors don't take kindly to the cheeky student who tosses outside information into his answer. The professor chose to exclude certain information from what she covered in class, and you should respect her choice. Especially on an exam she's grading.

## ✦ Sample Outline

Sometimes the easiest way to learn how to do something is to have an example. The following is an example of how your outline could look, give or take a lot of variables such as your outlining style, the amount of detail you want to include, etc. This outline is a guide, not a required format. You can and should tailor your outlines to your needs. So that you can see what a difference style makes, however, this outline follows all of the style rules, such as adhering to standard outlining form, using your typeface options and numbering the elements of rules of law. The better your outline looks, the easier it will be to learn the information it contains.

### CRIMINAL LAW

There are two sources of criminal law: *common law* and *statutes*. All federal criminal law is statutory. State criminal law varies from state to state; some crimes are statutory, some are common law.

Criminal statutes are always construed in favor of the defendant (D). A newer statute overrides an older one. Crimes are punishable under the law as it existed at the time the crime was committed.

Crimes are classified by the punishment they warrant: *Felonies* are punishable by death or imprisonment for more than one year. All other crimes are *misdemeanors*.

The reasons for imposing criminal punishment are:
1. incapacitation,
2. rehabilitation,
3. deterrence, and
4. retribution.

I.    <u>COMPONENTS OF A CRIME</u>.

To prove a crime, the DA must prove two concurrent elements:
1.    a voluntary physical act, and
2.    the requisite mental state.

A.    PHYSICAL ACT

A *physical act* includes:
1.    a voluntary bodily movement, or
2.    the failure to act if:
      a.    there is a duty to act,
      b.    D knows of the circumstances triggering the duty to act, and
      c.    D reasonably could perform the duty.

The duty to act can arise from:
1.    statute,
2.    the relationship between the D and the victim (V),
3.    because D created the peril, or
4.    from D's assuming the duty.

B.    MENTAL STATE—COMMON LAW

Under common law, there are four different mental states:

1.    <u>Specific Intent</u>.
      *Specific intent* is the intent to do the particular act. The jury cannot infer specific intent just by the commission of the act. Specific intent is judged by a subjective standard.

2.    <u>Malice</u>.
      *Malice* is the reckless disregard of a serious risk that harm will result from the D's action. Judged by a subjective standard.

3.    <u>General Intent</u>.
      The jury can infer *general intent* just by the commission of the act. Judged by a subjective standard, general intent means that D was aware:
      a.    that he was doing the act, and
      b.    the likely consequences of the act.

4.    <u>Strict Liability</u>.
      D can be found guilty just by doing the act, even if D is not fully aware of all the circumstances constituting the crime. Judged by an objective standard.

### C.   MENTAL STATE—MODEL PENAL CODE

The Model Penal Code uses the four following mental states:

1.   <u>Purposely</u>.
*Purposely* means D's conscious object is to do a particular act or cause a particular result. Judged by a subjective standard.

2.   <u>Knowingly</u>.
*Knowingly* means D knows or is aware that his conduct will very likely cause a particular result. Judged by a subjective standard.

3.   <u>Recklessly</u>.
*Recklessly* means consciously disregarding an unjustifiable risk of harm. Judged by a subjective standard.

4.   <u>Negligently</u>.
*Negligently* is the failure to appreciate a substantial and unjustifiable risk. Judged by an objective standard.

## II.   <u>HOMICIDE</u>.

### A.   COMMON LAW

1.   <u>Murder</u>.
The elements of *murder* are:
1.   the unlawful killing of a human being
2.   with malice aforethought.

*Malice aforethought* exists if:
1.   there are no defenses, and
2.   D acted with one of the following states of mind:
   a.   intent to kill,
   b.   intent to do grave bodily harm,
   c.   reckless disregard of a risk of death or great bodily harm, or
   d.   intent to commit a felony.

2.   <u>Felony Murder</u>.
The elements of *felony murder* are:
1.   the unlawful killing of a human being
2.   during the commission of or attempt to commit a dangerous felony.

Test:
1.   felony must be dangerous,
2.   D must be guilty of the felony,
3.   felony must be a separate crime from the homicide,
4.   felony must be one that forseeably could result in death,

     5.   death must have been caused during the commission of the felony or the immediate flight from the crime scene, and

     6.   the V is not a co-felon.

3.   <u>Voluntary Manslaughter.</u>

*Voluntary manslaughter* is "heat of passion" killing. Provocation can reduce a murder charge to voluntary manslaughter if:

1.   D was actually provoked,

2.   the provocation would cause sudden and intense passion,

3.   in the mind of an ordinary person,

4.   which causes him to lose control,

5.   there was no time to cool off between the provocation and the homicide, and

6.   D did not cool off between the provocation and the homicide.

4.   <u>Involuntary Manslaughter.</u>

The elements of *involuntary manslaughter* are:

1.   the unlawful killing of a human being

2.   with criminal negligence or in the process of committing an unlawful act.

<u>Note</u>: If the unlawful act is a dangerous felony, it's felony murder. If it's any other felony or a misdemeanor, it's involuntary manslaughter.

## B.   MURDER STATUTES

Statutory definitions of homicide separate homicides into first and second degree murder.

1.   <u>First Degree Murder.</u>

The elements of *first degree murder* are:

1.   the unlawful killing of a human being

2.   with premeditation and deliberation, or during the commission of one of the felonies listed in the statute.

Remember, "no time is too short to premeditate and deliberate."

<u>Note</u>: The test for felony murder is clearer under the statute than at common law—homicide is felony murder only if the felony committed is one of those listed in the statute.

2.   <u>Second Degree Murder.</u>

All murders that are not first degree murders are *second degree murders*.

## C.   CAUSATION REQUIREMENT

D's act must have caused the death of V. *Causation* is determined by looking at the four following factors:

1. <u>Cause in Fact</u>.
   Cause in fact is satisfied if but for D's act, V would not have died.

2. <u>Proximate Cause</u>.
   Proximate cause is satisfied if death is a probable consequence of D's act.

3. <u>No Superseding Intervening Causes</u>.
   D is liable for all foreseeable risks created by his act. Only unforeseeable, superseding intervening causes will break the chain of causation.

4. <u>Year and a Day</u>.
   V must die within a year and a day of D's act for D to be charged with homicide.

## III. CRIMES AGAINST THE PERSON.

### A. BATTERY (general intent crime)

1. <u>Simple Battery</u>.
   The elements of *simple battery* are:
   1. unlawful use of force
   2. resulting in injury to or offensive touching of V.

2. <u>Aggravated Battery</u>.
   The elements of *aggravated battery* are:
   1. unlawful use of force
   2. resulting in injury to or offensive touching of V
   3. with a deadly weapon, which results in grave bodily harm, or V was a woman, child or police officer.

### B. ASSAULT (specific intent crime)

1. <u>Simple Assault</u>.
   The elements of *simple assault* are:
   1. the attempt to commit a battery, or
   2. to create a reasonable apprehension in the mind of V of immediate bodily injury.

2. <u>Aggravated Assault</u>.
   The elements of *aggravated assault* are:
   1. the attempt to commit a battery, or
   2. to create a reasonable apprehension in the mind of V of immediate bodily injury,
   3. with a deadly weapon, or
   4. with the intent to maim or rape.

C. **RAPE** (general intent crime)

The elements of *rape* are:
1. unlawful sexual intercourse with another
2. without consent.

1. Sexual Intercourse.
   Any penetration at all is enough.

2. Consent.
   Lack of consent can be shown by any of the following:
   a. V incapable of consenting
   b. D threatens V with grave bodily harm, or
   c. D uses force.

3. Marital Rape.
   Some states still require the common law element that the intercourse be between unmarried individuals, but most states have done away with that element and recognize marital rape as a crime.

D. **STATUTORY RAPE** (strict liability crime)

No need to show intent, and there are no defenses. The elements are:
1. the carnal knowledge of a person
2. under the age of consent.

E. **KIDNAPPING** (general intent crime)

1. Simple Kidnapping.
   The elements of *simple kidnapping* are:
   1. unlawful confinement of a person, and
   2. either movement or concealment of V.

2. Aggravated Kidnapping.
   The elements of *aggravated kidnapping* are:
   1. unlawful confinement of a person, and
   2. either movement or concealment of V
   3. for ransom or some other unlawful purpose.

IV. THEFT CRIMES.

A. **LARCENY** (specific intent crime)

The elements of *larceny* are:
1. taking, and
2. carrying away
3. the property of another in possession
4. without consent
5. with the intent to deprive of permanently.

To be larceny, V must be in possession of the property when D took it. And, D must have had the intent to deprive V permanently of the property at the time he took it. So borrowing, mistaking something as your own property is not larceny.

B.  **EMBEZZLEMENT** (specific intent crime)

The elements of *embezzlement* are:
1. the fraudulent
2. conversion
3. of the property of another
4. by a person in lawful possession of that property.

Embezzlement is the bank teller who raids the till. D is in lawful possession of the money, has specific intent to defraud and convert the money to his own use.

C.  **FALSE PRETENSES** (specific intent crime)

The elements of *false pretenses* are:
1. obtaining title
2. to the property of another
3. by an intentional misrepresentation of a past or present fact
4. with the intent to defraud another.

V must really be deceived by the misrepresentation and his deception must be the reason why he gives title to D.

And, the misrepresentation cannot be regarding something that will occur in the future (a past or present fact only), so false promises don't count.

D.  **LARCENY BY TRICK** (specific intent crime)

The elements of *larceny by trick* are:
1. obtaining possession
2. of the property of another
3. by an intentional misrepresentation of a past or present fact
4. with the intent to defraud.

If D gets possession of the property, it's larceny by trick. If D gets full title to the property, it's false pretenses.

E.  **BURGLARY** (specific intent crime)

The elements of *burglary* are:
1. breaking and
2. entering
3. the dwelling of another

4. at night
5. with the intent to commit a felony inside.

Most states have both abandoned the night element and extended the crime to include structures other than dwellings. Breaking does not require damage to occur.

F. **ROBBERY** (specific intent crime)

Robbery is basically larceny plus the use of force. The elements of *robbery* are:
1. taking
2. the property of another
3. from the other person or his vicinity
4. by force or threat of grave bodily harm to V, a person with V, or V's family
5. with the intent to deprive of permanently.

G. **ARSON** (malice crime)

The elements of *arson* are:
1. burning
2. the dwelling
3. of another.

Most states extend the crime to include structures other than dwellings. Total destruction is not necessary—charring is enough.

## ✦ Dicta Column

The foregoing lesson on outlining should have allayed most of your outlining fears. Here are a few more things not to worry about.

✦ *Don't worry about what anybody else's outline looks like.* You already know this—outlines are personal. Some people like to have the security of a big giant outline. Others can't deal with anything longer than forty pages. Your outline is yours. Don't compare it to anybody else's.

✦ *Don't worry if you don't love all your outlines.* Some outlines turn out better than others, and you will like certain outlines more than others. That's the way it is. It doesn't mean that the outlines you like less aren't helpful—all your outlines will help you, because you condensed, organized and thought about the material.

✦ *Don't junk outlines and start over.* If three-quarters of the way through doing your outline you find that you wish you'd structured it differently or you don't like the way it looks, do not junk the outline and start over. You have to live with it, because you don't have time to start over. If you really think it's necessary, go back and fix up the outline the best you can by doing minor repair work, then keep moving forward. If you expect the outline to be perfect, you'll never be finished by the time exams roll around.

CHAPTER NINE

# ✦ Preparing for Exams

After classes end and before exam week begins, you will get some time off as a study period, which most schools call "reading week." Reading week can last anywhere from a few days to a week or more. Reading week is a time when you have no classes to go to and no assignments to complete. During reading week, all you have to do is study.

On the days leading up to reading week, however, you will have a whole list of things to do. You'll go to your last classes and do your last (and sometimes incredibly long) reading assignments. You'll outline that reading and add it to your outlines. You'll hand in your last legal research and writing assignment. You'll go to the library and photocopy all the old exam questions and answers that your professors put on reserve for you to practice on.

When reading week finally comes, all that activity comes to a grinding halt. After running around for days trying to tie up all the loose ends of the semester, you will find yourself with only one thing to do—study. Sounds simple, doesn't it? You'll just get up on the first day of reading week and start studying, right?

Ideally, the answer is yes. You should get up on the first day of reading week and start studying. For various reasons, however, many students don't do that. The transition from running around doing errands to sitting down at the desk and studying can be a difficult one. Many students are tired at the end of the semester and are not able to resist taking a little time off. Even the most industrious students can be tempted to procrastinate when they have days and days with nothing to do but study. Procrastination may take the form of marathon phone calls to classmates or a "Planet of the Apes" marathon on cable. Finally, even if you are in an industrious mood on the first day of reading week, you may find yourself skipping around between your subjects, putting in a lot of hours but never really feeling like you've learned anything.

How can you avoid these pitfalls? By having a plan worked out by the time reading week arrives. If you have a plan, you can jump right in and be

103

productive from the very first day of reading week. To make your plan, you need to map out how you will spend the days you have to study, both during reading week and on days between exams. This chapter will show you how.

# I. The Plan

Your plan is simple: You need a schedule. You need to schedule how you will spend your reading week days, your exam days and the days you have off between exams. When exams are about a month away, take half an hour to make your schedule. You'll need a calendar, some scratch paper and a thumbtack.

## A. Step #1: Make Your Calendar

Find a blank calendar and tear out the month when your exams are given (usually, December or May). Next, on the calendar write the name of the exam on the day it is scheduled. Those days are Exam Days. All you do on exam days is take exams. You do not study. Once your Exam Days are marked on the calendar, notice how many days you have in between exams. These are your Study Days. All you do on Study Days is study. You may have one day in between exams, you may have as many as three. Next, count up how many days you have for reading week. These too are Study Days. Finally, write down your total number of Study Days on your scratch paper.

## B. Step #2: Determine How Many Study Days Each Subject Requires

Not all your classes require the same amount of study time. You understand some subjects better than others. Some of your classes are worth more credits than others. For one reason or another, you may have studied less for one class during the semester than you did for the others. Keep these factors in mind as you divvy up your Study Days between your subjects. On the scratch paper, designate the number of Study Days you think each class requires.

## C. Step #3: Fill in the Calendar

Now you need to assign what subjects you will study on each particular day. It's easier to start at the end and work backwards, because during exam week the rule is that on the day or days before any exam, you may study that subject and that subject only. You need to think about that subject and nothing else on the days before the exam. So fill in the days before and between exams first.

Now fill in your reading week days. How you spend these days is up to you. The only guideline is that you want to limit the number of subjects you study on any given day to not more than two. The reason is that you need time to really immerse yourself in a subject. If you flit back and forth between all your subjects in a single day, you never give yourself the chance to see how much you can learn when you really spend time with a subject.

Also, if your professor offers a review session, by all means put it on your calendar and plan to attend. Sometimes these sessions can be incredibly helpful, and sometimes they can be a complete waste of time. You will know which it is within a few minutes of sitting down. If you learn something, great. If you don't find the session helpful, leave.

## D. Step #4: Put Your Calendar on the Wall Where You Can See It

Take your thumbtack and pin your schedule to the wall. Don't worry too much about whether this is your end-all be-all schedule. If you decide that one subject needs more or less attention, you can modify your plan when exams get closer. What matters most is that your plan is ready for you when reading week arrives, and you can jump right in and start studying. Each day that you accomplish what you set out to do that particular day, cross the day off on your calendar. You're one step closer to vacation.

# II. How to Spend Your Study Days

You're in law school—you already know how to study. But no matter how well you study, there are traps that students can fall into in their first semester, and you want to avoid them. The way to avoid them is to think about how you will spend your study time, so you can spend it as wisely as possible.

## A. Study Days

Absolutely unstructured, your Study Days allow you to study however and whenever you want. To make the best use of your time, it's a good idea to think about four questions: where, when, how and what you will study.

### 1. Where

Different people study different places. Some people need the solitude of home to get anything done, while others would spend a day at home on the telephone or watching television. Some people like the structure of the library, with the hard chair and fuzzy ambient noise of fellow studiers. Other people like real noise, need to be around activity and do their best work in a busy café. You know who you are. Study where you will know you will get the most work done. If that's a café, fine—don't switch to library-studying now just because you think that's where you "should" be studying.

### 2. When

Again, people are different. Some people are morning people, others are night people. Study when you are most alert, energized and ready to learn. The only thing to think about is what time your exam starts. Don't get used to sleeping until noon every day if your exam is scheduled to begin at 8:00 a.m.—you'll be groggy.

### 3. How

Because you're not used to the solitude of reading week, it's a natural reaction to want to congregate with other people to study, but watch out. Unless you have been studying with a study group all semester, this is not the time to start studying with other people. By the time reading week comes, it's too late in the day to meld into a workable group. You all have different ways of studying. You all have somewhat different levels of proficiency in the subject. You should neither waste your time teaching the rest of the group things they should already know nor scare yourself to death by talking to people who act like they know a lot more than you do. Studying is rare at these last-minute study groups. Commiseration is much more likely, because the truth is, students band together for comfort, not to learn anything. For all these reasons, you're better off being strong and going it alone. If you feel the need to ask someone questions, just call a friend and ask.

### 4. What

You'll no doubt be happy to know that the answer to the question "what should you study?" is not "everything." You've been studying "everything" all semester. You went to class. You took notes. You consulted study aids, read your casebooks and briefed your cases. Congratulations—you're done with all that now. You don't have to look at your casebooks or class notes ever again. Why? Because now is the time to limit your focus to your outline. Your outline contains every important thing that you learned over the entire semester, so that's all you need now. Learn the outline and you'll learn everything you need to know.

The first thing you should do as you start to study for each class is read your outline from beginning to end. Think hard about it as you go. When you're finished, read it again. As you continue going through your outline over and over, you will become more and more familiar with it. You'll be able to say the elements of a crime without looking at the page. You'll remember the test for personal jurisdiction. You'll know the format of your outline so well that you'll be able to turn to a specific section effortlessly. By the time you are finished studying for your exam, you will have put your outline to memory.

Only consult outside sources if you have a question that your outline doesn't answer. If you have a question, find the answer in a study aid or your notes, your casebook or a friend, make a note of it in your outline and move on. Don't spend any more time with the outside source than it takes to answer the question. Limit your focus to your outline.

## B. Days Before Exams

Days before exams are the last chance you have to study. It seems like these days would be your most grueling study days, but the opposite is actually true. You already know what you need to know. You've been studying all semester. You condensed and organized an entire semester of information into an outline and you put that outline to memory. You're already prepared to take your exam.

Therefore, days before exams are more about getting your mind ready for the exam than they are about studying for ten hours. You should go through your outline once on the day before the exam, just to get familiar with it, but the bulk of your time should be spent doing two things: (1) taking practice exams and (2) getting ready for anything.

### 1. Taking Practice Exams

Taking practice exams and evaluating your answer is the best way to get ready to take your exam. If you haven't read the following chapter on exam-writing skills, now is the time to do it. You need to be familiar with the exam-writing rules and conventions at least a few weeks before exams begin. The rules will be fresh in your mind, and you can practice applying them when you take your practice exams.

To get the most out of taking practice exams, you need to take them seriously. Set aside a few hours to devote solely to the practice exams. Turn off your telephone ringer and get a clock to time yourself. Treat the questions as if they really were your exam questions and try to write the best answers you can. Don't do so many questions that you exhaust yourself, but do as many as you need to get comfortable with the subject matter, say two or three. If your exam is open-book, use your outline to answer the practice exam question. It will help you familiarize yourself with the outline and help you locate what you need quickly and efficiently.

When you're finished, read over your answers. Notice all the positive aspects of your answer, and congratulate yourself for the good arguments you made. Also take note of the things you forgot to include. Think about how you approached the question, how readable your answer is and whether you repeated yourself. Look to see whether you followed the exam-writing lessons of Chapter Ten.

Now look at the model answer. A word of caution, however: In comparing your answer to the model answer, do not be too hard on yourself. The model answer is just what it sounds like—it is either the one the professor wrote himself as a recommended answer or the very best answer in the class. Your answer does not have to be "model"; it just has to be better than most of your classmates'.

Use the model answer constructively by looking at it objectively to see how the writer approached the problem, how many issues he discussed and how thoughtful the discussion was. Think about what your professor liked about this answer. Use the model answer as a guide rather than a standard to which you compare your answer. The model answer may discuss some issues that you did not. Your discussion of some issues may be more in-depth than the model answer's. It doesn't matter. As you will see in Chapter Ten, everybody answers exams differently, and two answers that are completely different can nonetheless receive exactly the same grade. More importantly, exams are graded on a curve. To score well, you do not need to write a perfect or model answer. You just need to write a better answer than a good percentage of your classmates.

Once you have finished a couple of practice exams and have read over your answers, stop. Close your outline and put down your pen. It's time to stop studying.

### 2. Getting Ready for Anything

For some, calling it a day can be difficult. If there's time left to study, first years tend to think that's what they should be doing. To make sure you stop studying, you should fill the rest of your day keeping your hands busy doing practical things to ready yourself for your exam. You are already mentally prepared for your exam. Now it's time to play boy scout and prepare yourself physically. Your goal is to be ready for anything, and here's your checklist:

+ *Set out all the materials you need to take to the exam.* If the exam is closed-book, that means you only need to take your outline. You can't use it, but having it there in your backpack to answer any right-before-you-go-into-the-exam-room questions will be very comforting.

  If the exam is open-book, bring everything. Bring your outline, your case book, your class notes and case briefs, study aids if your professor allows them, and anything else you can think of. You won't consult any of these things except your outline—you won't have time—but having tons of material around you is a security blanket. You'll have the comfort of knowing that you can't be stumped by any exam questions, because you'll be able to find the answer somewhere, no matter what it is. Also, your classmates will be intimidated by the sight of all your resources stacked up around you, and intimidated classmates are always a good thing come exam time.

+ *Gather up your essentials.* Take something to drink into the exam room (just watch out for a caffeine overload). Bring something to eat if you're someone who needs to eat often. Bring some pain reliever in case you get a blinding headache in the middle of the exam. Same goes for stomach ailments. Put a pair of earplugs in your backpack if you're sensitive to noise. Even if you're not sensitive, you might want to bring a pair of earplugs anyway, because you never know how you're going to feel in the middle of an exam. They may help your concentration, and they certainly will block out the person with the sniffles sitting behind you. Pack a sweatshirt in case the room is cold. Bring more of your favorite pens than you could go through in a month. In short, bring it all. The truth is, you probably won't use half the stuff you bring, but you want to be prepared.

+ *Wear a watch.* There's probably a clock in the room, but what if it's broken? Remember, the goal is to be prepared. It's essential that you know what time it is throughout your exam, so wear a watch.

+ *Bring any outside materials that your professor recommended.* Consult a friend in your class to confirm whether your professor suggested you bring any special items to the exam, such as a calculator or handout from class.

+ *Pack your backpack.* Once you've gathered all these items, pack your backpack. Double check that you've got everything. Then set out your most comfortable outfit. Bring layers of clothes, so that you'll be comfortable if the heating or air-conditioning goes on the blink. Finally, set your alarm clock. Then set a backup alarm clock. One of the alarms should not be electric, in case your electricity goes out. This sounds paranoid, but knowing that your alarm is foolproof will help you get some sleep.

+ *Exercise.* On the day before an exam, you should get some exercise. If you exercise regularly, do whatever you normally do—run, swim, play basketball, whatever. If you don't normally exercise, go for a half-hour walk. The goal here is physically and mentally to get away from your outlines and clear your head.

+ *Relax.* When you're all done, sit down and relax. Do whatever it is you do to get your mind off law school, whether it's watching television or listening to music, reading a book or just having a beer (notice we say a "beer," not a "twelve pack"). Relax and rest your mind. Then go to bed and try not to think about the exam you have the next day. Remember, you are prepared, both in mind and body. You are ready for anything.

## + Dicta Column

As with every aspect of law school, there a few things you do not need to worry about as you go into exam week:

+ *You're nervous.* Don't worry about being nervous? No. Do not worry about being nervous, because a certain amount of nervousness is not only to be expected, but healthy. If you weren't nervous, you weren't taking law school seriously. Moreover, a bit of nervousness actually helps your performance on exams by giving you that extra push you need to excel.

✦ *Do not worry that everybody studied harder/knows more than you do.* As you already know, how much time your classmates spend studying has little or no correlation to how much they actually accomplished or learned. Thinking is the key to learning in law school. You have been thinking, so even if it looks like everybody has been studying twice as much as you, don't worry about it. It doesn't mean anything. Similarly, if you talk to a classmate before the exam and he talks as if he knows a lot more than you do or has a better understanding of the class, don't worry about it. As with the amount of hours a person studies, talk means nothing. Just ignore it and focus on yourself.

✦ *That you'll freeze up and forget everything.* It's not going to happen. You've packed too much into your head to forget it all spontaneously; it's simply not possible. If you do find yourself panicking during the exam, however, don't just sit there. Get up and walk down the hall for a few minutes. Take a deep breath and have a drink of water. Just getting out of the exam room will calm you down more than you can imagine. Take a minute and look out the window. Try to have a little perspective. Yes, law school is important, but it's not the end of the world. You know what you need to know to do well on your exam. So calm down, go back to your chair and start writing.

CHAPTER TEN
# ✦ Writing Exam Answers

For all your work in each class, you will receive one grade—your grade on the final exam. You spend an entire semester reading, briefing, outlining and studying in preparation for that one exam. Because you know you have only one opportunity to demonstrate everything you've learned, exams are a daunting prospect for any law student.

The truly frightening thing about law school exams, however, is that even if you learn everything there is to know about a particular subject, you can nonetheless receive an average or even a low grade on your final exam. It happens at every law school every year. When first semester grades come out, many students are not only disappointed by their grades, they're baffled. These are students who studied all semester, read the material, outlined each class and knew the law. They knew the answers to the exam questions. Yet after all that, they received mediocre or even substandard grades. How is that possible?

They didn't know how to write exam answers. The truth about exams is that knowledge is worthless if you do not also know how to write a good exam answer. Knowing how to write a good exam answer is just as important as knowledge of the subject matter. Remember that.

"But I'm a terrible writer," you're saying. It doesn't matter. You don't have to write well to get good grades on your exams. You have to write smart. Writing smart means, above all else, being clear. Your professors want clarity over eloquence. Write smart and make your exam easy to read.

To write smart you need to learn the three essential elements of clarity:

I.  Common sense
II. Style
III. Substance

This chapter will show you how.

# I. Common Sense

First, the easy part. There are seven ways to dramatically increase your chances of receiving good grades on all your exams, and none of them require any knowledge of the law. They require common sense. Think about it. Exams are over. For you, it's the first vacation you've had in months. For your professors, it's time to work. While you relax at home with friends and family, your professor has a towering stack of blue books staring at her. If she opens your exam, potentially the ninety-seventh she's read that day, and sees a maniacal scrawl defacing the first page, unreadable and scratched out, wrinkled and smeared from tears of desperation, how do you think she feels? Not like giving you a good grade, we can tell you that much.

Shocking as it may be, a lot of exams look that bad and worse. After all your work over the past semester, is it really wise to jeopardize your final grade by being lazy? A big part of writing smart is just using common sense and knowing that you need to make your professor like you as soon as she opens your blue book. You can increase your chances of receiving a good grade just by being considerate and using common sense. The eight rules are:

## A. Write Legibly

Write fast, of course, but write as neatly as you possibly can given your time constraints. If your handwriting is truly abysmal, type your exams. Most law schools allow this. If you do plan to type your exams, you should type your practice exams as well to make sure you type as fast as you think you can.

## B. Write on One Side of the Page

Would you want to read pages that are soaked through with ink from the other side? Only write on the front side of the page in your blue book, please. Be selfish for once. The trees will forgive you.

## C. Skip Lines

Double spacing is easier to read, no matter how neat your writing. And, the more blue books you use, the more you had to say, right?

## D. Number Your Blue Books

Before you do anything, write your exam number (usually your social security number) on the front cover of several blue books. After writing your exam, help your professor keep track of your answers and do not risk one of your blue books getting lost in the shuffle by numbering your blue books in sequence. For example, if you used three blue books, write on the front of the books "1 of 3," "2 of 3" or "3 of 3."

## E. Use Headings

Be as clear as you possibly can. When you begin discussing a new topic, skip a line, start a new paragraph, make up a heading and underline it. It doesn't have to be a good heading; certainly do not give it more than two seconds' thought. Just write down what your paragraph will be about, underline it, and begin writing the paragraph.

## F. Keep Your Paragraphs Short

Remember Chapter Eight's outlining lesson. Bite-sized chunks of information are easier to process. The easier your answer is to understand, the more points you get. So keep your paragraphs to four or five sentences, tops.

## G. Don't Overdo It

Do not get caught up composing a nice essay. This is not high school, and a law school exam is not an essay. It's an exam; it's not supposed to be perfect. Do not spend time coming up with just the right word. If you make a mistake, cross it out neatly and write what you meant to say. You do not have time to wad up your blue book and start over, so don't.

## H. Take Shortcuts

There is no reason for you to spend time re-writing the names of the parties in your exam question. Take a smart shortcut and use the universal abbreviations for plaintiff and defendant: "P" and "D." For example, let's say "Katie" is bringing suit against "Jack." The first time you mention these people in your answer, write "Katie, the plaintiff (P), will bring suit against Jack, the defendant (D)." From then on, Katie is "P" and Jack is "D."

# II. Style

A bit more sophisticated than the common sense rules above, these style guidelines are the backbone of writing smart. You can know all the law in the world, but if you ignore the following rules, your grade will suffer. The six style rules are:

## A. Argue Both Sides

Even if the exam question begs for you to slant your answer one way, don't. It's a trap. The fact pattern where the destitute old lady signs a contract with the con-man for life insurance has been around since the beginning of time. Be wary. More importantly, be neutral. No matter what, do not let your emotions get the better of you. Write an answer that gives fair representation of both sides of the dispute. Even if one party appears to be the sure loser or is morally repugnant, you must look hard at the question from that party's point of view and build the best argument you can for him. You will get points for doing what your classmates found themselves unable to do—come up with reasonable, solid, even creative arguments for the poor guy who doesn't have a chance.

## B. Hedge Your Bets

As you make arguments for both sides of the lawsuit, remember to hedge your bets. Even if one side clearly has the better argument, do not decide unequivocally that he is sure to win. Your conclusion should be littered with words such as perhaps, maybe, might, probably, likely, could, would, should. You can't know for certain how a judge or jury would decide the dispute. You are not a judge or jury; you're a lawyer. Lawyers always hedge their bets.

## C. Do Not Repeat Yourself

No matter how astute the point you're making, you only get points for saying it once. Writing it twice wastes your time and dilutes your professor's appreciation of your brilliance.

## D. Be Fearless

Unless your professor tells you otherwise, the general rule is that professors give points for correct arguments but do not deduct points for misguided ones. The theory is that in legal argument, there are no truly wrong answers. So be fearless. Write down every argument you can think of. Apply an ancient legal doctrine to a modern situation. Be imaginative and creative. Be interesting. Look at the question as an open invitation. The only things to remember are to begin with the basic arguments (the "rule"), then move to the creative argument, use common sense and stay within the subject matter. No professor wants to read about Contract law on a Torts exam.

## E. Try to Finish the Exam

Without short-changing your treatment of each part of the question, make a real effort to finish your exam. Often there will be less competition towards the end of the exam, because so many students run out of time and aren't able to answer all the questions. Further, finishing your exam shows your professor that you can manage your time even in the most stressful situations, which can only increase your chances of a better grade.

## F. Use "Because"

"Because" is a magic word for purposes of exam answers, because it reminds you to explain yourself. "Because" reminds you to tell your professor why a legal theory applies. Writing the word "because" reminds you to weave facts from the exam question into your answer. When you write a sentence like "P has a cause of action against D," follow with the word "because," and you will be reminded to tell your professor why P has a cause of action against D. "Because" forces you to show your professors that you are thinking like a lawyer, and that is what they want to see.

# III. Substance

Last but not least, substance. Your exam is your chance to showcase all the knowledge you've accumulated over the course of the semester. The more you know, the better off you'll be, probably. But the clearer you are, the better off you'll be, certainly. While knowledge is important, clarity is vital. All the knowledge in the world is useless if your professor cannot understand your answer. Whatever the amount of knowledge you've accumulated over the semester, you must present that knowledge in a clear format. You must write smart.

There are two steps to presenting your knowledge clearly: reading the question and writing your answer following IRAC.

## A. The Question

Everybody knows you have to read the question, right? Yes, everybody knows you have to read the question. But people don't read the question. They skim over the question once. Then in a panic, they jump into their blue books, scribbling on every line, writing what will end up to be one twenty-five-page paragraph of an answer. And worse, they write on both sides of the page.

You know better than that. As you sit there in the exam room, you must remind yourself to read the question, slowly and carefully. When you finish, read the question again. Read quicker this time, making a list in the margin of every issue you see. When you have finished the second reading, stop for at least a minute and think about the question. Gather your thoughts. What is the question asking? Figure out what is really at stake, who the parties are and what legal theories could apply. Create a picture in your mind.

You may at this point want to take a couple of minutes and write a very loose, bare-bones outline of how you will structure the answer. Keep it simple, however; just note the issues you will discuss, maybe some applicable law, and that's it. Do not get over-involved in outlining and lose track of time. You do not get points for making a nice outline. You get points for writing a good answer from that outline. When you have gathered your thoughts and you understand the question, pick up your pen.

## B. The Answer

You've read the question. The pen is in your hand. Now comes that moment of silent panic. Where are you supposed to start? The blank page staring at you and the clock ticking in the background don't help you decide. You know you are wasting valuable time, but you are paralyzed. You can't decide where to start.

You can avoid allowing that moment of panic to become five minutes of panic by remembering one simple rule: It doesn't matter where you start. All that matters is that you write an exam answer that follows IRAC: Issue, Rule, Analysis, Conclusion. You remember IRAC from legal writing. You start with an issue. It doesn't matter which one.

### 1. Issue

Most exam questions have multiple issues. Torts exams are sometimes "issue spotting" exams where you earn points for seeing all the ways to impose liability on as many people as possible. Do not let it overwhelm you. If you are worried about forgetting issues once you've spotted them, make small notes on the question to remind you. Then pick an issue and start writing.

This is where your headings come in. If the first issue on your Contracts exam is whether, under the facts, there is an offer, that's your heading: "Whether there is an offer," or "Is there an offer?" Just write something about offer and underline it. Then underneath your heading, start writing. "The first issue to address is whether under these facts there is an offer." Use facts from the question that suggest whether there is or is not an offer. For example, "Joey, the defendant (D), told Gina, the plaintiff (P), that he thought P's house needed painting. The issue is whether this could be construed as an oral offer by D to paint P's house."

Remember that although it doesn't matter in what order you choose to address the issues, it does matter how much time you allot each issue. Some issues clearly will be more important than others, and you must devote more time to discussing them. Important issues are more complicated and require more detailed treatment, and spending extra time with an important issue shows your professor that you recognize the relative importance of the issues presented by the question.

A good approach is to begin with the obvious issues. You want to make sure you cover the basic, obvious issues because this is where a lot of points come from. Only after you've dealt with the basic issues should you move on and try to be creative about your issue spotting and answering.

Finally, remember what subject you're working in. If you're taking a Torts exam, don't even consider whether you see a Contracts or Civil Procedure issue. Your exams test you on one subject and one subject only. Your professors do not want to read about any subject but the one they taught you.

### 2. Rule

Once you have stated the issue, write down the applicable rule. Paraphrase the rule from memory or, on an open-book exam, you can copy the rule straight from your outline. If you happen to remember a case name that stands for that rule of law, write it down, but case names are not required on exams.

### 3. Analysis

Analysis does not mean writing something along the lines of "there are good arguments on both sides but P should win." That is what professors call "conclusionary" and you will get no points for that answer. Analysis means looking at the issue from both sides of the dispute and making good arguments for each side by applying the facts from the question to the applicable rule to decide the issue. Analysis on an exam literally tracks your thought process; in your mind you are evaluating the dispute by applying the facts from the question to the law that you learned over the course of the semester to settle the issue presented by the question.

The way to do well on exams is to write down your thought process, step by step. A good answer never misses a beat or skips a step in the analysis. Never say to yourself, "The professor already knows that. I won't waste my time writing it down." This is where you lose points. Write your answer as if your reader knows nothing, about the question or the law. If you assume your reader is ignorant, it will force you to write down everything you know and every step in your analysis process. Writing down your thought process is the only way you can show your professor that you know how to analyze a problem.

A good way to organize your analysis section is to use separate paragraphs for each party's arguments. As you think about the problem, put yourself in each side's shoes. Say you're the plaintiff. Look at the problem from the plaintiff's perspective and write down all the arguments the plaintiff will make. In the next paragraph, be the defendant. Respond to all the plaintiff's arguments and throw in a few of your own. That's analysis.

### 4. Conclusion

Once you have exhausted the plaintiff and defendant's possible arguments, it's time to conclude. This is the only place that your exam IRAC model differs from legal research and writing. On exams, your conclusion should be less certain than in a legal memorandum. On exams, you really have to hedge your bets.

"Conclusion" on an exam means a short paragraph weighing the relative chances each side has for success. If one side has a stronger argument then definitely say so, but do not go so far as to say that side will definitely win the case. Just evaluate the chances each side has of success and suggest a possible outcome. Then it's time to move on to the next issue.

Work through the exam, issue by issue, until you get to the end. When you have finished, skim your answers and add thoughts in the margin if you need to. Do not pore over your answers; just skim them once and turn in your blue book. Going back and re-thinking your answers after you have finished your exam is not a good idea, because the first answer that came to you is almost certainly your best. Just turn in your blue book. That's it. You're done.

## ✦ Dicta Column

Exams are probably the most stressful time of the entire semester. As always, however, there are several things you do not need to worry about as you go through exam week:

✦  *Do not be unnerved by post-exam comparison talk.* Immediately after the exam, you will see students congregating to discuss how they answered the exam. It's human nature to compare, and many people in your class will talk about the entire exam, question by question, discussing every one of their answers to the questions.

   If you choose to join the conversation (and we recommend that you don't), then prepare to be unnerved. You invariably will hear that people wrote different things than you did, which will make you question your performance on the exam. Even if you felt okay about your exam when you turned it in, all the talk about answers and issues and rules will make you think you forgot to include the most important points.

   If you decide to join the exam-discussion, remember this: Nothing that your classmates say has any bearing on the grades your professor will award the exams she reads. Think about all the elements of writing smart—common sense, style and substance. A classmate who tells you after the exam that she included five legal theories in her answer that you hadn't even thought of will not necessarily do better than you. Did she use common sense? Argue both sides? Was she conclusionary? Did she hedge her bets? Did she skip lines?

The factors that go into exam evaluation go beyond what students tell you they wrote on the exam. There is no way for you to know what kind of answer anyone in your class wrote. How they wrote their answer is as important as what they wrote. You know that. So remember that if you choose to engage in post-exam comparison talk.

✦ *Do not worry if you feel like you failed the exam*. One of the biggest mysteries about law school exams is that how you think you did on the exam has absolutely no correlation to the grade you will receive. The student who literally feels sick as she turns in her blue book can get the highest grade in the class. Law professors grade exams in relation to all the other exams in the class. Because you have no idea how your classmates did, there is absolutely no way you can gauge how well you did.

✦ *Do not worry about studying for your next exam*. The best part of exam week is that after constant studying for weeks on end, you get to take a break. Once you finish each exam, take the rest of the day and night off. Go out to dinner, see friends, go to the movies. Whatever you do, do not study. Now is not the time. Now is the time to reward yourself for your accomplishment. Law school is a marathon, not a sprint. Exams are exhausting. You need to give yourself time to recuperate and pace yourself so that you can perform well on all your exams.

✦ *Do not worry about your grades during your vacation*. You've been worried all semester. The last thing you should worry about as you go on vacation is your grades. You won't know how you did until you come back for the next semester of law school. In fact, you will probably have to wait longer to get your grades because most professors will not have finished grading exams by the time the new semester begins. Just enjoy your vacation and don't worry about law school. Trust us, it'll be there when you get back.

# ✦ Glossary

abate: to reduce, diminish, or entirely destroy.

abet: to aid or encourage another.

abrogate: to cancel or revoke.

A.C.L.U.: the American Civil Liberties Union.

actus reus: the physical act of committing a crime.

ad hoc: for a particular purpose.

adjudge: to judicially decide.

affiant: person who gives an affidavit.

affidavit: a written declaration of facts confirmed by oath of the affiant.

amicus curiae: friend of the court.

arguendo: for the sake of argument.

assumpsit: a common law action based on a contract.

at bar: before a court.

bona fide: in good faith.

capacity: legal competence, either age or fitness.

caveat emptor: let the buyer beware.

certiorari: the U.S. Supreme Court uses a writ of certiorari to determine which cases it wishes to hear.

chancery: equity court, the relief given by an equity court.

chattel: item of personal property (as opposed to real property); includes animate and inanimate items.

civil action: any suit that is not a criminal case.

collateral: noun: property that secures a debt; adjective: related to, supplemental.

common law: the body of law that is derived from judicial opinions.

criminal law: defines certain conduct as criminal and defines the punishment to be imposed for such conduct.

de facto: in fact or in deed.

de jure: in law or by law.

deposition: a discovery tool whereby an attorney asks oral questions to the deponent, who answers under oath. The written transcript of the testimony is also called a deposition.

dicta: observations and opinions in a case that are extraneous to the case and have no precedential weight.

discovery: the means by which parties to a lawsuit gather information from the other side to prepare for trial.

equity: derived from English law, equity is a system of justice separate from common law, its object being fairness and justice. Our courts have both legal and equitable powers, and administer equitable relief alongside legal relief.

ex parte: one-sided, by one party, or for the benefit of one party only.

express: definite, declared or written, not ambiguous.

fee simple: complete title to real property.

force majeure: force outside the parties' control, such as fire, earthquake, flood; an act of God.

foreseeable: a reasonable person could appreciate the possible consequences.

guaranty: a promise to pay the debt of another person should that person fail to pay.

habeas corpus: a writ of habeas corpus contends that a defendant is being unlawfully deprived of his freedom, i.e., is being unlawfully imprisoned.

heretofore: legalese for "before."

immunity: exemption from something the law requires of citizens.

implied: indirect, implied, or inferred; the opposite of "express."

inchoate: not completed, partial.

indictment: written and sworn accusation charging a person with the commission of some offense.

in personam: proceedings instituted against the person.

in rem: proceedings against the thing itself, i.e. naming the property itself as the defendant in a foreclosure action.

interrogatories: a discovery device by which written questions are given to a witness who attests to their truth.

intestate: to die without making a will.

judicial notice: when a court takes as true a certain fact even though neither party has provided evidence to support the fact.

jurisprudence: the philosophy of law, the science of law.

laches: when a party unreasonably neglects to assert a claim, an equity court can bar the claim under the doctrine of laches.

lis pendens: a pending lawsuit; a court's control over property involved in the lawsuit until final judgment.

material: important or necessary.

mens rea: a guilty mind.

parol: oral, as opposed to written.

per curiam: "by the court"; denotes a legal opinion authored by the whole court as opposed to a single judge or justice.

petitioner: party who instigates an equity proceeding or who appeals from a judgment; same thing as a plaintiff or appellant.

plea: old word for a pleading.

pleadings: formal written claims of parties to a lawsuit.

preemption: doctrine which provides that federal law preempts or overrides state and local laws.

presumption: an inference that a certain fact is true.

prospective law: applies only to acts which are done after the enactment of the law.

punitive: punishment, penalty.

quantum meruit: "as much as deserved"; paying a reasonable estimation of the value of what was received.

quid pro quo: "something for something."

reasonable person: a hypothetical everyman, a person with human faculties and failures, of average intelligence and reason.

recidivist: a repeat offender, a habitual criminal.

rescission: annulment, nullification.

res ipsa loquitur: "the thing speaks for itself"; a doctrine which infers negligence on the defendant's part by the mere facts that the instrumentality causing harm was in the defendant's sole control and the injury was one that doesn't normally happen in the absence of negligence.

respondeat superior: "let the master answer"; doctrine whereby superiors are liable for the acts of their employees.

respondent: responds to a petitioner's claim; same thing as a defendant or appellee.

retroactive law: a law that applies to actions that were done in the past as well as present and future acts.

sine qua non: an absolute requirement or necessity.

slip opinion: a decision of a court that is published as a separate leaflet before it is printed in the reporters.

stare decisis: to follow decided cases.

subpoena: an order requiring someone to appear to give sworn testimony regarding a particular case.

testate: dying with a will.

testimony: evidence given by a witness who is competent and under oath.

third party beneficiary: person for whose benefit an agreement is made but who is not a party to the agreement.

Uniform Commercial Code: code which governs commercial transactions, such as sales, leasing, and the transfer of goods, funds and securities.

unilateral: one-sided, by one party or for the benefit of one party only.

United States Attorney: prosecutes and defends the U.S. Government in all civil suits in which it is involved.

usury: charging an illegally high rate of interest.

verdict: formal decision made by a jury.

waiver: intentionally giving up a legal right.

with prejudice: an action dismissed with prejudice bars the subsequent re-filing the same cause of action at a later date.

without prejudice: an action dismissed without prejudice allows the subsequent re-filing of the cause of action at a later date.

writ: a court order requiring someone to do something or giving authority to have it done.

# ✦ Index